# TOURISM MANAGEMENT - I

## TRAVEL AND TOURISM

## CHEF SATHISH KUMAR SOMASUNDARAM

*Dedicated to Hotel Industry & Staff*

# Contents

# Foreword

Welcome to the study of a dynamic group of industries that have developed to serve the needs of travellers worldwide – tourism! Tourism is the business of travel. Whether we are travellers or we are serving traveler's needs, this exciting and demanding group of visitor services industries touches all our lives. In this unit you will understand the different perspectives on the study of tourism, know the meaning of the term 'tourism', 'visitor', 'tourist', 'excursionist', 'transit traveller' and the difference between travel and tourism. You will also come to know of different definitions adopted by different countries on the term 'tourist'.

The subject of travel is exciting and fascinating. Human beings have been moving from place to place for about 5 million years. Our early ancestors, Homo erectus, originated in eastern and southern Africa. But remains of these same forms of early humankind have also been found in China and Java. It has been estimated that migrations of this type took about 15,000 years, but this is a brief span of time in the long history of humanity. Various theories have been proposed regarding the motivation for such amazing journeys. Foremost is that these wanderings were in search of food and to escape from danger. Another theory is that people observed the migrations of birds and wanted to know where the birds came from and where they were going. Recently, in the most dramatic discovery of its kind ever made, the preserved body of a man dubbed the "iceman," who died 5,000 years ago, was found in the ice in mountainous northern Italy. Some of the scientists studying his body and accoutrements have concluded that he was returning to his home in what is now Switzerland from a journey to the south of what is now Italy. Since the times of the wanderings of ancient peoples, we have been traveling in ever-widening patterns about the earth. From the days of such early explorers as Marco Polo, Ibn battute, Christopher Columbus, Ferdinand Magellan, and James Cook to the present, there has been a steady growth in travel. Tourism is one of the world's most rapidly growing industries. Much of its growth is due to higher disposable incomes, increased leisure time and falling costs of travel. As airports become more enjoyable places to pass through, as travel agency services become increasingly automated, and as tourists find it easier to get information on places they want to visit, tourism grows. The Internet has fuelled the growth of the travel industry by providing on line booking facilities. It has also provided people with the power to explore destinations and cultures from their home personal computers and make informed choices before finalizing travel plans. With its immense information resources, the Internet allows tourists to scrutinize hotels, check weather forecasts, read up on local food and even talk to other tourists around the world about their travel experiences for a chosen destination. This new trend has made the tourism job very challenging. The holiday makers want a good rate of return on their investment. They are to be lured with value additions and improved customer service. This also put emphasis on the regular flow of manpower with specific skills at the appropriate levels to match and cater to global standards. The success of the hospitality industry comes from provision of quality rooms, food, service and ambience. There is no doubt that fitness has increasingly become a larger part of everyone's life. And business and leisure travellers alike look to maintain their fitness goals while away from home. Awareness should be created about the environment and education. A collective effort and co-operation with powerful networking are the need of the hour. People should be acting as the watchdogs of the society as far as environmental issues are concerned. Eco-tourists are a growing community and tourism promotions have to adopt such eco-practices which could fit this growing community.

# Preface

Knowledge, which mainly comes through education, helps us to get extensive exposure of many things and beliefs. Obviously, the clearer the vision, more is the understanding; which, in turn, is somehow assists us to have optimistic outlook and this positive attitude affects our tourism related decision making process, thus, resulting in increased travel propensity. In addition to this psychological dimension, education also improves employment opportunities, which ensures economic freedom, this is accountable for income enhancement resulting in more disposable income and we have already discussed the consequential dimensions in the previous paragraph.

# Acknowledgements

We would like to acknowledge the help of all the people involved in this Book and, more specifically, to the authors and reviewers that took part in the review process. Without their support, this book would not have become a reality.Our sincere gratitude goes to the chapter's authors who contributed their time and expertise to this book.I wish to acknowledge the valuable contributions of the reviewers regarding the improvement of quality, coherence, and content presentation of chapters. Most of the authors also served as referees; we highly appreciate their double task.

I wish to thank my College and Management (NASC Family)
Chef Sathishkumar Somasundaram
Assistant Professor
Department of Catering Science and Hotel Management
Nehru Arts and Science Collage –Coimbatore

R.Prahadeeswaran
Head of Department
Department of Catering Science and Hotel Management
Nehru Arts and Science Collage –Coimbatore

# Prologue

The international "responsible tourism" movement, born in the 1970s in response to negative impacts of tourism are campaigning and linking with a wide spectrum of community groups and the public and private sectors. Growing numbers of organizations that are outside of predominantly travel industry are also re-thinking their role in tourism and creating strategies for change. Farmers, women, Indigenous Peoples, human rights, activists, civil society, are organizing together to share common concerns. Many of these global movements involve travel and transit, financial transactions, and a reliance upon tourism industry that are all ultimately targets of change. These individuals and movements must recognize the role they play, the power they have to demand changes, and design clever strategies to use tourism as a catalyst for change. Some of these groups are organizing solidarity tours to pressure oppressive governments and supports each other at the grassroots, some are voluntarily linking with each other on social justice issues. There is also growth in nature travel and ecotourism, an area that immediately involves local people and can be a catalyst. Currently, thousands of communities around the world are attempting some form of tourism development. While some communities are creating strategies for resistance to tourism, many people in communities where abrupt development transformations are taking place have little information about the forces transforming their lives. What is apparent, though, is that most of the communities are going through almost entirely the same process fairly defined cycles of expectations and disappointments. Yet, tourism continues to grow haphazardly, often to the detriment of local people, communities and the environment, with little long-term, integrated planning. We have been following development paths that promote unlimited economic growth. This westernized model of growth have been applied, often believing, sometimes unwillingly, and increasingly resistant, to other countries in India

# ONE
## TOURISM INTRODUCTION

What is Tourism? When we think of tourism, we think primarily of people who are visiting a particular place for sightseeing, visiting friends and relatives, taking a vacation, and having a good time. They may spend their leisure time engaging in various sports, sunbathing, talking, singing, taking rides, touring, reading, or simply enjoying the environment. If we consider the subject further, we may include in our definition of tourism people who are participating in a convention, a business conference, or some other kind of business or professional activity, as well as those who are taking a study tour under an expert guide or doing some kind of scientific research or study. These visitors use all forms of transportation, from hiking in a wilderness park to flying in jet to an exciting city. Transportation can include taking a chairlift up a Colorado mountainside or standing at the rail of a cruise ship looking across the blue Caribbean. Whether people travel by one of these means or by car, motor coach, camper, train, taxi, motorbike, or bicycle, they are taking a trip and thus are engaging in tourism. That is what this block is all about-why people travel (and why some don't) and the socioeconomic effects that their presence and expenditures have on a society. Any attempt to define tourism and to describe its scope fully must consider the various groups that participate in and are affected by this industry. Their perspectives are vital to the development of a comprehensive definition. Four different perspectives of tourism can be identified: 1. The tourist: The tourist seeks various psychic and physical experiences and satisfactions. The nature of these will largely determine the destinations chosen and the activities enjoyed. 2. The businesses providing tourist goods and services: Business people see tourism as an opportunity to make a profit by supplying goods and services that the tourist market demands.It is precisely the significance of the word 'tour' which forms the root of the word 'tourism'. The international dictionary of tourism, published in 1953 by the international academy of tourism at Monte Carlo, points out that tour in English and in French means a journey, a circulative trip. The nineteenth century dictionary defines tourist as "people who travel for pleasure of traveling, out of curiosity; and because they have nothing better to do", and even " for the joy of boating about it afterwards".

1. The tourist: The tourist seeks various psychic and physical experiences and satisfactions. The nature of these will largely determine the destinations chosen and the activities enjoyed.

2. The businesses providing tourist goods and services: Business people see tourism as an opportunity to make a profit by supplying goods and services that the tourist market demands.

3. The government of the host community or area: Politicians view tourism as a wealth factor in the economy of their jurisdictions. Their perspective is related to the incomes their citizens can earn from this business. Politicians also consider the foreign exchange receipts from international tourism as well as the tax receipts collected from tourist expenditures, either directly or indirectly.

4. The host community: Local people usually see tourism as cultural and employment factor. Of importance to this group, for example, is the effect of the interaction between large numbers of international visitors and residents. This effect may be beneficial or harmful or both.

**1.1** Tourism: Thus, tourism may be defined as the sum of the phenomena and relationships arising from the interaction of tourists, business suppliers, host governments, and host communities in the process of attracting and hosting these tourists and other visitors. Tourism is a composite of activities, services, and industries that delivers a travel experience: transportation, accommodations, eating and drinking establishments, shops, entertainment, activity facilities, and other hospitality services available for individuals or groups that are traveling away from home. It encompasses all providers of visitor and visitor-related services. Tourism is the entire world industry of travel, hotels, transportations, and all other components, including promotion that serves the needs and wants of travelers. Finally, tourism is the sum total of tourist expenditures within the border of a nation or a political subdivision or a transportation-centered economic area of contiguous states or nations. This economic concept also considers the income multiplier of these tourist expenditures. One has only to consider the multidimensional aspects of tourism and its interactions with other activities to understand why it is difficult to come up with a meaningful definition that will be universally accepted. Each of the many definitions that have arisen is aimed at fitting a special situation and solving an immediate problem, and the lack of uniform definitions has hampered study of tourism as a discipline. Development of a field depends on

(1) Uniform definitions
(2) Description
(3) Analysis
(4) Prediction and
(5) Control.

Modern tourism is a discipline that has only recently attracted the attention of scholars from many fields. The majority of studies have been conducted for special purposes and have used narrow operational definitions to suit particular needs of researchers or government officials; these studies have not encompassed a systems approach. Consequently, many definitions of "tourism" and "the tourist" are based on distance traveled, the length of time spent, and the purposes of the trip. This makes it difficult to gather statistical information that scholars can use to develop a database, describe the tourism phenomenon, and do analyses. The problem is not trivial. It has been tackled by a number of august bodies over the years, including the League of Nations, the United Nations, the World Tourism Organization (WTO), the Organization for Economic Cooperation and Development (OECD), the National Tourism Resources Review Commission, and the U.S. Senate's National Tourism Policy Study. The following review of various definitions illustrates the problems of arriving at a consensus. We examine the concept of the movement of people and the terminology and definitions applied by the World Tourism Organization and those of the United States, Canada, the United Kingdom, and Australia. Later, a comprehensive classification of travelers is provided that endeavors to reflect a consensus of current thought and practice.

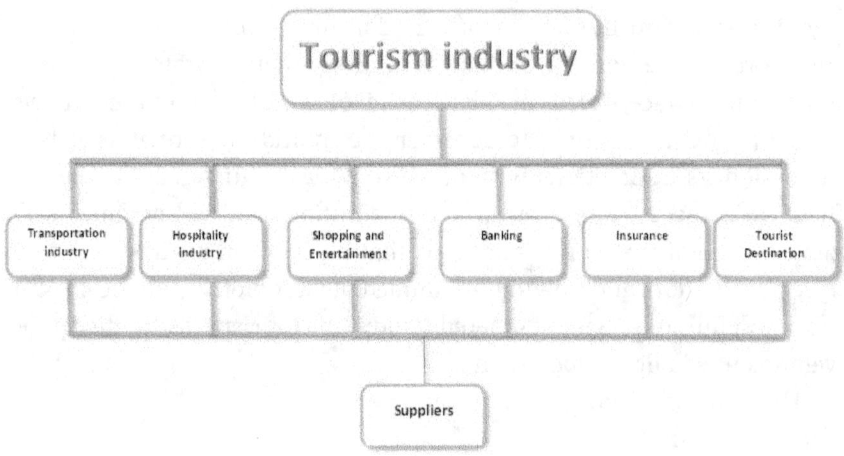


http://recreation-tourism.blogspot.com/2011/04/tourism-industry.html

**1.2 World Tourism Organization** : The International Conference on Travel and Tourism Statistics convened by the World Tourism Organization (WTO) in Ottawa, Canada, in 1991 reviewed, updated, and expanded on the work of earlier international groups. The Ottawa Conference made some fundamental recommendations on definitions of Tourism,

travellers, and tourists. The United Nations Statistical Commission adopted WTO's recommendations on tourism statistics on March 4, 1993. Tourism: WTO has taken the concept of tourism beyond a stereotypical image of "holiday making." The officially accepted definition is: "Tourism comprises the activities of persons traveling to and staying in places outside their usual environment for not more than one consecutive year for leisure, business and other purposes." The term usual environment is intended to exclude trips within the area of usual residence and frequent and regular trips between the domicile and the workplace and other community trips of a routine character. Main Characteristics of Tourism identified from the Definition:

1. Tourism arises from a movement of people to, and their stay in, various destinations.

2. There are two elements in all tourism: the journey to the destination and the stay including activities at the destination.

3. The journey and the stay take place outside the usual place of resident and work, so that tourism gives rise to activities, which are distinct from those of the resident and the working population of the places, through which th tourist travels and in which they stay.

4. The movement to destinations is of temporary, short term character, with the intention of returning to the usual environment within a few days, weeks or months.

5. Destinations are visited for purposes other than taking up permanent resident or employment remunerated from within the places visited.

The international union of official travel organization (IUOTO), new called world tourism organization (WTO), has defined tourist as a temporary visitor staying for at least twenty four hours in a country visited when the purpose of the journey can be classified under one of the following headings;

(a) leisure recreation, holiday, health, study, religion and sports; or

(b) business, family, mission meetings. Travelers staying less than twenty – four hours according to WTO are 'excursionists'.

Conceptually, tourism arises from the movement of people to, and their stay in, different destinations. The 'journey' is the dynamic element in it and the 'stay', static. The 'journey' and 'stay' are to, and in, destinations outside the normal place of residence and work. Destinations are visited for purpose not connected with paid work or regular employment. Again, this movement is of a temporary and short duration a few days, weeks or months.

Within the parameters of the above definitions, tourists would mean those traveling for pleasure, domestic reasons, health, business purposes, conferences, meetings, diplomatic and religious purpose plus arrivals on cruise, even though they do not involve overnight stay. Persons not to be considered 'tourists' and the individuals transiting through a country, those coming to take up a residence, those who live in one country but cross over to another to work.

1. Visitors who spend at least one night in the country visited
2. Foreign air or ship crews docked or in lay over ad who used the accommodation establishments of the country visited
3. Visitors who do not spend at leas one night in the country visited although they may visit the country during one day or more and return to their ship or train to sleep

4. Normally included in excursionists. Separate classification of these visitors in nevertheless preferable
5. Visitors who come and leave the same day
6. Crews who are not residents of the country visited and who stay in the country for the day
7. When they travel from their country and stay in the country visited for the day
8. Who do not leave the transit area of the airport or the port. In certain countries, transit may involve a stay of one or more. In this case they should be included in the visitor statistics
9. Main purpose of visit as defined by the Rome conference

**Classification of Tourism**

1. Recreational: Recreational or leisure tourism takes a person away from the routine of everyday life. In this case, people spend their leisure time at the hills, seas, beaches etc.

2. Cultural: Cultural tourism satisfies the cultural and intellectual curiosity and involves visits to ancient monuments, places of historical or religious importance, etc.

3. Sports/Adventure: Trips have taken by people with a view to playing golf, skiing and hiking, fall within this category.

4. Health: Under this category, people travel for medical, treatment or visit places where there are curative possibilities, for example, hot springs, spa yoga, etc.

5. Convention Tourism: It is becoming an increasingly important component of travel. People travel within a country or overseas to attend conventions relating to their business, profession or interest.

6. Incentive Tourism: Holiday trips are offered as incentives by major companies to dealers and salesmen who achieve high targets in sales. This is a new and expanding phenomenon in tourism, These are in lieu of cash incentives or gifts, Today incentive tourism is a 3 billion dollar business in the USA alone

**Nature of Tourism**

1. It is a service-based industry.
2. It is a dynamic sector.
3. It can be described in term of supply and demand.

**Planning Supply**

• Various modes of transportation and other tourism-related infrastructure.

• Accomodation.

• Tourist information.

• Marketing and promotion.

• The community of communities within the visitor's destination area.

• The political and institutional frameworks for enabling tourism.

**Importance of Tourism**

• Employment Generating It creates a large number of jobs among direct services providers (such as hotel, restaurants, travel agencies, tour operators, guide and tour escorts, etc.) and among indirect services providers (such as suppliers to the hotels and restaurants, supplementary accommodation, etc.)

• Infrastructure Development Tourism spurs infrastructure development. In order to become an important commercial or pleasure destination, any location would require all the necessary infrastructure, like good connectivity via rail, road, and air transport, adequate accommodation, restaurants, a well-developed telecommunication network, and, medical facilities, among others.

• Foreign Exchange The people who travel to other countries spend a large amount of money on accommodation, transportation, sightseeing, shopping etc. Thus, an inbound tourist is an important source of foreign exchange for any country. Impact of Tourism Economic Social Cultural Environmental Benefits Costs Benefits Costs Benefits Costs Benefits Costs

• Generates local employment

• Stimulates profitable domestic tour-related industries.

• Generates foreign exchange for the country and injects capital and money into the local economy.

• Helps to diversify the local economy.

• Improves infrastructure.

• Increases tax revenues from.

• Higher demand created by tourism activity may increase the price of land, housing and a range of commodities necessary for daily life.

• Demands on health services provision and police service increase during the tourist seasons at the expense of the local tax base.

• Enhances economic diversification through tourism.

• Provides Recreational and cultural facilities local communities as well as visitors. • Develops and enhances public space.

• Enhances local community's esteem and provides cross cultural understanding.

• Possible inability of local amenities and institutions to meet service demands. • Without proper planning, it increases litter, vandalism, and crime.

• Overcrowding and traffic congestion.

• Disrupts traditional community ways of life.

• Changes community structure and culture to meet tourism demands.

• Enhances local cultural awareness.

• Generates revenue to fund the preservation of archaeological sites, historic buildings, and districts.

• May share of cultural knowledge and experience to revive local traditions and crafts.

• Youth begin to emulate the speech and attire of tourists.

• Historic sites can be damaged through tourism development and pressures.

• There can be long term damage to cultural traditions and the erosion of cultural values, resulting in cultural change beyond a level acceptable to the host destination.

• Creates parks, nature preserves, ecological preservation..

• Improves waste management.

• Increases awareness and concern for the environment.

• A negative change in the physical integrity of the area.

• Rapid development, over-development, and overcrowding can forever change the physical environment and ecosystems of an area. • Degradation of parks and preserves. Industries Related To Tourism • Transporta)on It is the movement of people and goods from one place to another. A well-developed transport industry, as well as infrastructure, is integral to the success of any travel and tourism enterprise.

**Industries Related To Tourism**

• Travel Agencies A travel agency is a retailing business that sells travel related products and services, particularly package tours, to customers on the behalf of suppliers such as airlines, car rentals, cruise liners, hotels, railways, and sightseeing. Travel agencies play a very important role as they plan out the itinerary of their clients and make the necessary arrangements for their travel, stay, and sightseeing, besides facilitating their passport, visa, etc.

• Tour Operators A tour operator assembles the various elements of a tour. It typically combines tour and travel components to create a holiday. Tour operators play an important role in the travel and tourism industry.

• Tourist Destinations A tourist attraction is a place of interest for tourists, typically for its inherent or exhibited cultural value, historical significance, nature or build beauty or amusement opportunities. These are the basic fundamentals of the tourism industry.

**Industries Related To Tourism**

• Cultural Industries Cultural or creative industries are responsible for the creation, production, and distribution of goods and services that are cultural in nature and usually protected by intellectual property rights. As tourists like to visit places of cultural significance and soak in the culture of the area, the cultural industry is very important to travel and tourism.

• Leisure, Recreation, and Sport Leisure or free time is a period of a time spent out of work and essential domestic activity. Recreation or fun is spending time in a manner designed for healing refreshment of body or mind. While leisure is more like a form of entertainment or rest, recreation requires active participation in a refreshing and diverting manner. Tourism Products

• A tourism/tourist product can be defined as the sum of the physical and psychological satisfaction it provides to tourists, during their traveling and temporary stay and on the way to the destinations.

• A tourism product includes five main components such as physical plant, services, hospitality, freedom of choice, and a sense of involvement.

**Characteristics Of Tourism Products**

1. Intangible: Tourism is an intangible product means tourism is such kind of product which can not be touched or seen and there is no transfer of ownership, But the facili:es are available for specified :me and for a specified use. For e.g. a room in the hotel is available for a specified :me.

2. Psychological: The main mo:ve to purchase tourism product is to sa:sfy the psychological need a@er using the product, by geAng experience while interac:ng with a new environment. And experiences also mo:vate others to purchase that product.

3. Highly Perishable: Tourism product is highly perishable in nature means one can not store the product for a long :me. Produc:on and consump:on take place while a tourist is available. If the product remains unused, the chances are lost i.e. if tourists do not purchase it. A travel agent

or tourism operator who sells a tourism product cannot store it. Produc:on can only take place if the customer is actually present. And once consump:on begins, it cannot be stopped, interrupted or modified. If the product remains unused, the chances are lost i.e. if tourists do not visit a par:cular place, the opportunity at that :me is lost. It is due to tourism reason that heavy discount is offered by hotels and transport genera:ng organiza:ons during the offseason. Characteris*cs Of Tourism Products

4. Composite Product: Tourist product is a combination of different products. It has not a single entity in itself. In the experience of a visit to a particular place, various service providers contribute like transportation The tourist product cannot be provided by a single enterprise, unlike a manufactured product.

5.Unstable Demand: Tourism demand is influenced by seasonal, economic, political and others factors. There are certain times of the year which see a greater demand than others. At these times there is a greater strain on services like hotel bookings, employment, and the transport system, etc.

**1.3 Travelers:**

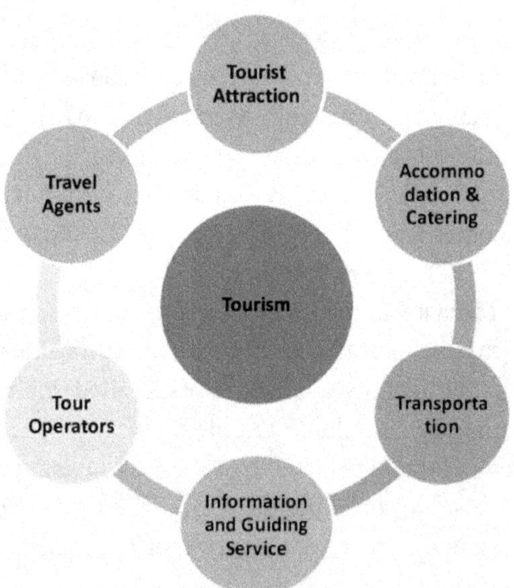


https://forestrybloq.com/different-components-of-tourism-marketingupdated/

- Traveler Terminology of International Tourism
- Underlying the foregoing conceptualization of tourism is the overall concept of
- traveler.
- Traveler is defined as "any person on a trip between two or more countries or
- between two or more localities within his/her country of usual residence."
- Travelers may be included in tourism statistics or may not be. All types of travelers
- engaged in tourism are described as visitors, a term that constitutes the basic
- concept of the entire system of tourism statistics.
- Visitors are persons who travel to a country other than the one in which they
- generally reside for a period not exceeding 12 months, whose main purpose is other
- than the exercise of an activity remunerated from within the place visited.

**Visitors are subdivided into two categories:**

1. Tourists, i.e., temporary visitors staying at least twenty four hours in the country visited and the purpose of whose journey can be classified under one of the following headings:

(a) Leisure (recreation, holiday, health, study, religion, and sport);(b) Business, family, mission, meeting.

2. Excursionists, i.e., temporary visitors staying less than twenty-for hours in the country visited (including travellers on cruises). The above definition excludes travellers who, in the legal sense, do not enter the country (e.g., air travelers who do not leave an airport's transit area – Transit Visitor).The drawback of definition of a Visitor as per WTO is that it does not talk about visits made within the country. For these purposes a distinction is drawn between a

### 1.4 Nature of Tourism

- It is a service-based industry.
- It is a dynamic sector.
- It can be described in term of supply and demand.
- Tourists from core genera9ng markets are iden9fied as the demand side

· Supply side includes all facili9es, programmers, a?rac9on, and land uses designed and managed for the visitors

· Tourism planning should strive for a balance between demands and supply.

· This requires an understanding not only of market characteris9cs and trends but also of the planning process to meet the market needs

## 1.5 DOMESTIC AND INTERNATIONAL VISITOR

**Domestic Visitor:**

A person who travels within the country he is residing in, outside the place of his usual environment for a period not exceeding 12 months.

**International Visitor:**

A person who travels to a country other than the one in which he has a usual residence for a period not exceeding 12 months.

**Cruise Passenger:**

He is a visitor who arrives in the country aboard cruise ships and who does not spend a night in an accommodation establishment in the country.The broad class of travelers categorized as migrants, both international and domestic, is also commonly excluded from tourism or travel research. They are excluded on the grounds that their movement is not temporary, although they use the same facilities as other travelers, albeit in one direction, and frequently require temporary accommodation on reaching their destination. The real significance of migration to travel and tourism, however, is not in the one-way trip in itself, but in the long-run implications of a transplanted demand for travel and the creation of new travel destinations for separated friends and relatives.

Notes:

(1) Visitors who spend at least one night in the country visited.

(2) Foreign air or ship crews docked or in lay over and who use the accommodation establishments of the country visited.

(3) Visitors who do not spend at least one night in the country visited although they may visit the country during one day or more and return to their ship or train to sleep.

(4) Normally included in excursionists. Separate classification of these visitors is nevertheless recommended.

(5) Visitors who come and leave the same day.

(6) Crews who are not residents of the country visited and who stay in the country for the day.

(7) When they travel from their country of origin to the duty station and vice-versa (including household servants and dependents accompanying or joining them).

(8) Who do not leave the transit area of the airport or the port? In certain countries, transit may involve a stay of one day or more. In this case, they should be included in the visitor statistics.

(9) Main purposes of visit as defined by the Rome Conference (1963).Other groups of travellers are commonly excluded from travel and tourism studies because their travel is not affected by travel promotion, although they tend to compete for the same types of facilities and services. Students and temporary workers traveling purely for reasons of education or temporary employment are two leading examples. Another frequently excluded group consists of crews,

although they can be regarded as special subsets of tourists and excursionist.

## 1.6 Tourism-introduction

Defining tourism is not a simple matter, as it is a complex industry made up of many different businesses, the common theme being that they provide products and services to tourists/visitors.

Family sitting on grass at Trelissick Garden, Cornwall, England, UKAccording to the United Nations World Tourism Organisation (UNWTO), tourism entails the movement of people to countries or places outside their usual environment for personal or business/professional purposes. These people are called visitors. Generally speaking, a visitor is classified as a (same-)day visitor if their trip does not include an overnight stay and a tourist if it does include an overnight stay. The purpose of their trip can be for business, leisure or personal reasons, other than to be employed by a resident entity in the country or place visited.

If a trip's main purpose is business/professional, it is often subdivided into two further categories - 'attending meetings, conferences or congresses, trade fairs and exhibitions' and 'other business and professional purposes'.

## 1.7 TYPE OF TOURISM

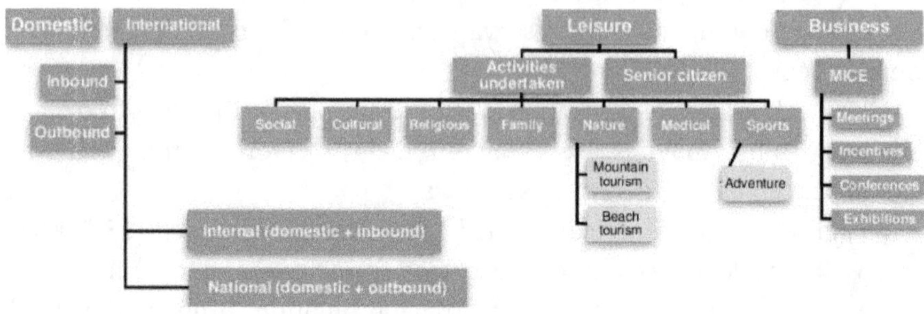


https://www.researchgate.net/figure/Types-and-Forms-of-tourism

There are three basic forms of tourism: domestic tourism, inbound tourism, and outbound tourism.Domestic tourism refers to activities of a visitor within their country of residence and outside of their home (e.g. a Brit visiting other parts of Britain).Inbound tourism refers to the activities of a visitor from outside of country of residence (e.g. a Spaniard visiting Britain).Outbound tourism refers to the activities of a resident visitor outside of their country of residence (e.g. a Brit visiting an overseas country).The tourism industry in Britain is primarily a private sector industry, consisting of around 200,000 businesses, some very large including international hotel groups and airlines, as well as small and medium sized businesses, industry groups and bodies.Domestic tourism is the core of businesses revenue (generally at least 80%, particularly outside of London), with demand peaking during the school holidays, particular Easter and Summer. Dealing with the demands of international visitors requires specialist knowledge, cultural understanding and investment.Most UK statistics separate spending and volume of day visitors from overnight tourists. Visit Britain's statistics and research reports focus on overseas visitors who come to Britain.

For domestic statistics (ie. data on people from within Britain who visit another location in Britain) get in touch with the tourism organisations for England, Scotland, Wales, Northern Ireland and London. "Tourism comprises the activities of persons traveling to and in places outside their usual environment for not more than one consecutive year for leisure, business and other purposes".

The report distinguishes the following types following types of tourism:

a. Domestic tourism involving residents of country visiting their own country
b. Inbound tourism involving residents of a country other than their own
c. Outbound tourism involving residents of a country visiting other countries. These three basics forms of tourism can in turn be combined to drive the following categories of tourism.

- Internal tourism which comprises domestic tourism and inbound tourism,
- National tourism which comprises domestic tourism and outbound tourism and
- International tourism which comprises in bound and outbound tourism

Relationship between 'Leisure', 'Recreation' and 'Tourism' the words 'Leisure', 'Recreation' and 'Tourism' is often used to express similar meanings.

What exactly is the relationship between these words?

Leisure is a measure of time left over after work, rest, sleep and household chores. Leisure is the time when an individual can do what he likes to refresh his/her spirits. Recreation means a variety of activities, which a person could to refresh his/her spirit. It may include activities as diverse as a game of golf, watching television or traveling abroad.

Tourism therefore, is simply one of these activities, which a person could undertake to refresh his/her sprite. It places tourism firmly as part of recreation activities spectrum of a person.

## 1.8 MOTIVATION FOR TRAVEL

Motivations for most travel have been fairly obvious – religion, economic gain, war, and escape migration. What is left travel for pleasure, which, is the most common form of travel in the modern world.

The following may be listed as motivation to travel.

**Education and culture**

a. To see how people I other countries live, work and play
b. To enjoy scenic beauty and cultural sight
c. To gain a better understanding of what goes on elsewhere
d. To attend special events/festivals/cultural function

**Relaxation and pleasure**

a. To get away from the routine of life
b. To have a good time away from home
c. To have a romantic or exotic expression

**Ethnic**

a. To go to places where one's family came from
b. To visit places where one's family or friend lived in the past

Indians settled abroad and holding foreign passports keep on coming to Indian again and again, swelling the number of tourist arrivals in India.

**Classification**

Tourism can be classified in to six distinct categories according to the purpose of travel.

1. Recreational:

Recreation or leisure tourism takes a person away from the humdrum of every day life. In this case, people spend their leisure time at the hills, sea beaches etc.

1. Cultural:

Tourism satisfies the cultural and intellectual curiosity and involves visits to ancient monuments, places of historical or religious importance etc.

3. Sports/Adventure:

Trips taken by people with a view to playing golf, skiing in the mountains or hiking, fall within this category.

4. Health:

Under this category, people travel for medical treatment or visit place where there are curative possibilities, for example, hot springs, spas, yoga, etc.

5. Convention Tourism:

It is becoming an increasingly important component of travel. People travel within a country or overseas to attend conventions relating to their business, profession or interest.

6. Incentive tourism:

Major companies offer Holiday trips as incentives to dealers and salesmen who achieve high targets in sales. This is a new and expanding phenomenon in tourism. These are in lieu of cash incentives or gifts. Today, incentive tourism is a 3 million dollar business in the USA alone.

**1.9 BARRIERS TO TRAVEL**

In spite of numerous factors listed above favoring the development of tourism, there are some that act as barriers to travel. These fall into following categories:

1. Cost:

People are subjected to monetary retrains and cannot afford the expense of travel. According to a study on the subject, in the United States alone, over 50% of people cannot undertake holiday travel due to high costs. In India, it is 90%.

2. Time:

This is characteristic neither of those who are nor in a position to leave their business or profession to take time off from work.

3. Health:

Many reasons, especially old people, cannot travel due to poor health and physical limitations.

4. Family:

Parents of small children are not in a position to travel due to the family responsibilities and inconveniences of travel.

5. Lack of interest:

Ignorance and lack of information about other places and other people can be a major barrier to travel.

## 1.10 FORMS OF TOURISM

Tourism can be divided in to different forms on the basis of length of stay type of transport used, price paid or the number of people in a group. From a geographical point of view, important distinctions are international and domestic tourism and long haul short haul tourism.

Domestic tourism includes those within there own country. Domestic tourism dose not involve use of foreign currency nor causes any balance of payment problem.

When people travel to a country other than own with different economic and political system, the movement becomes international tourism. It involves preparation of several documents – passport, visa, etc., - to cross the national boundaries of a foreign country. It also involves conversion of one's own currency to the currency of the country where one is traveling. It is also likely that visitor may face the problems of a language.

The size of a country determines the extent of international tourism. USA for instance is a very large country and has many domestic tourist attractions. Therefore, the extent of the international tourism is only 10% of the total tourism in the country.

Long haul tourism comprises journeys exceeding 5,000 kilometers – below that is termed short haul tourism. The distinction is relevant from the point of view of aircraft operations and marketing. Long haul tourism is very important for India because the majority of India's tourism is very journeys. Potential tourist markets of India are long haul. India's neighboring countries are not rich enough to take holidays on a large scale.

A further basic distinction in tourism relates to the purpose of visit – especially from the marketing point of view. Holiday tourism is what most countries try to promote. Other forms of tourism do not need much promotion.

Holiday tourism can be further subdivided in to sun, sand and sea type of tourism where beach – related open-air activities and good weather are important factors. The mountain tourism, like the Himalayan tourism, also comes under this category. The other is 'culture' and 'sightseeing' where the focus is on culture, history, art and architecture of a country. This tourism has a significant role in India's pattern of inbound tourism. Cultural tourism is a major tourism resource of the country.

Special interest tourism comprises those who visit a country for a common purpose, i.e. visiting a country for meting friends and relatives do not make heavy demands on the facilities and infrastructure of the country as they often stay with their relatives and friends.

Mass tourism – refers to the participation of a large number of people in tourism, i.e. millions of tourists visiting Spain, Italy or France, often out – numbering the residents. This is a phenomenon as yet limited to developed countries.

This category of the people who visit a country for business includes businessmen or professionals attending trade fairs, conventions and conferences, participants in the incentive travel offered by their companies and people coming to negotiate business deals and contracts.

Clearly, business is no leisure activity. Since the business visitors use the same facilities as the holidaymakers do, they are included in the category of 'tourists' or visitors.

## 1.11 TRAVEL INDUSTRY NETWORK

In the early years of this century, travel apparently was not looked upon as an industry as such but as a collection of businesses whose common link was to provide services to travelers.

Broadly, we can categories them in three ways:

1. Direct providers of services. Examples: airlines, hotel, ground transportation, travel agents, restaurants and retail shops.
2. The second category is support services to direct suppliers. Examples: specialized services such as tour organizers, hotel management firms, travel research organizations and travel trade publications. There may be other services too, such as food service contractors, laundry services, etc.,
3. The third category consists of developmental organizations that include planners, government organizations, financial institutions, vocational training institutes, etc.; they do not cater to day-to-day needs of travelers. Their plans may take years to fructify, such as the development of a resort, shopping complex for tourists or training of the staff for tourism – related enterprises.

## 1.12 TOURISM AND TOURISM PRODUCT

Ideally, tourism product is a package tour which comprises an air seat, accommodation at the lace to be visited, local transportation, sightseeing, entertainment, meals, shopping, etc., the production is composite in nature and includes everything a visitor purchases, sees experiences and feels from the time he/she leaves home until the time he/she returns.

The tourist product can be brought as a package as indicated above or separately. Airlines seat and hotels room are tourist products, which can be bought separately.

## 1.13 THE TOURISM PRODUCT

https://ihmnotessite.com/index.php/tour-travel-management

NEED FOR PLANNING DEVELOPMENT

The serious situation caused by haphazard development has made pole and the governments aware of the need for planning of tourism development based on scientific research of the requirements of the travel market and the capacity of the area to take in the tourists. The need for planning is paramount. We do not provide more seats to a plane or rooms in a hotel beyond its maximum capacity, taking into account the passenger's comforts.

Tourism is a form of social industrialization with all its advantages and disadvantages. Its advantages have to be grasped and utilized with care so that planning comes in. planning is of greater benefit to developing societies where tourism is a new phenomenon and has had little or no adverse effect so far.

a.  Planning should be integrated to avoid as far as possible, disparities in the standards of amenities for the visitors and local population.
b.  Tourism planning should not be left totally to private enterprise in search of profit government must actively participate in it.

Tourism has become a major industry in many countries of the world and has thus a pervasive effect on the economy of the nations as well as their social structure. Unplanned tourism can hamper a nation in getting maximum benefits from its development.

PLANNING PROCESS

Tourism is part of the services industry. Its importance economic and social – has to be balanced by a government in relation to the competing priorities of a nation.

A government must take a decision as to whether tourism is important for its economic, social and political interests. And if the decision is positive, planning based on in-depth research is imperative.

National Goals

Decisions at the national level have to be taken by the government, preferably in consultation with various interests involved. A national policy is called for incorporating the directions in which tourism development should take place. The policy should also spell to national goals and objectives.

National objectives could be as under:

1.  To develop infra and super structure to provide recreation facilities for visitors and the resident population.
2.  Preservation of cultural resources and the heritage.
3.  To maximize economic benefits in terms of improvements of standards of living of the people.
4.  Generation of new employment.
5.  Stimulation of development at regional levels.
6.  Ensuring development at tourist centers and resorts consistent with the needs of each area.
7.  Maximizing visitor's satisfactions.

**1.14** DEMAND AND SUPPLY

Tourism development is a complex phenomenon requiring in-depth study of resource and demand pattern in each country.

In Great Britain, a 1990 study revealed that 60 percent of domestic visitors go to the sea for their holiday, which is accessible in a few hours from any part of the country.

Some 10 million foreign visitors add to the congestion of London, annually along with another 15 million domestic visitors. In the case of France, the sea is also the focus of attention of the foreign visitors adding to the congestion on its beaches. The Italians refer the lakes, while the visitors opt for the history ad culture of Rome and many other cities of Italy spreading millions of visitors thinly all over the country.

Since India is a large country, it is in a position to distribute the tourists evenly though Delhi and Bombay have pressure in peak winter months.

The pattern of traffic has to be kept in while planning the development of tourism in a destination, especially at the supply side, as it is not flexible. Hotels are not built in a day nor are the airports. It tool Los Angeles several years to expand its airport to host the Olympics in 1984. For successful tourism planning, current and future supply has to be correlated to current and future demand.

**FACTORS INFLUENCING TOURISM DEVELOPMENT**

The following are some of the factors, which influence tourism development in a destination area:

1. Size of the existing population
2. Diversity and vitality of already existing tourist activity.
3. Whether the facilities were planned and planted in the area or grew simultaneously because of some man-made or national attraction.
4. Availability of land and finance
5. Impact on the local community-benefits and social costs
6. Attitude of the local people towards the tourism projects.
7. Magnitude and speed of development
8. State of the local economy – options of alternate development
9. Availability of local manpower – a dynamic population
10. Whether the area is extensive for future expansion or only limited expansion is possible.

WHAT CONSTITUTE TOURIST ATTRACTIONS

Planners must know what makes a tourist destination click. The following are some of the factors, which would create tourist attraction:

1.  Scenic

    a.  Natural beauty
    b.  Wildlife, flora and fauna
    c.  Attractive coastline/long beaches
    d.  Mountain location, rivers
    e.  Wildlife safari parks

2.  Cultural

    a.  Ancient building, archaeological sites, history ad culture.
    b.  Religion
    c.  Customs an traditions

3.  Way of Life

    a.  Folk arts
    b.  Handicrafts
    c.  Traditional and folk dances
    d.  Festivals/fairs
    e.  Art

4.  Entertainment and amusement

    a.  Theater, cinemas
    b.  Night life
    c.  Local leisure, good food
    d.  Health resort, spa, springs
    e.  Recreational/amusement arks
    f.  Sporting activities, adventure sports
    g.  Zoo and ocean marinas

5.  Climate

    a.  Mild temperature

b.   Hours of sunshine

Any or several of these attractions lure visits to a destination.
GOVERNMENT'S ROLE IN PLANNING OF TOURISM

To make a tourism plan work, government has to create a favorable climate for investment through regulations and fiscal measures. Since most private investors would expect a reasonable return on investment, special financial incentives are necessary to make tourism investment attractive. A tourism project needs to be assisted at two stages: first at the time of making investment, and subsequently at the operational stage. Participation in the development of a tourism plan by government offers direct financial subsidy.

In India, industrial Finance Corporation of India (IFCI) at central level and State Financial Corporation at state level finance hotels, on the recommendation of the Department of Tourism.

India tourism Finance Corporation (TFCI) was created to finance tourism projects and it is doing a good job. Other organization also continues to finance tourism projects.

The government can help tourism planning through manpower development by running hotel and tourism training schools/courses. Finally the extent of government concessions to tourism is basically liked with the importance a state attaches to the tourism sector compared to other sectors of economy.

TOURISM PLANNING IN INDIA

Source - https://en.wikipedia.org/wiki/
Ministry_of_Tourism_%28India%29

Development had to begin with the provision of basic infrastructure, especially at importance places of tourist interest where there were little or no facilities. The plan was divided into three parts. Part – I schemes dealt with the development of accommodation at places of international tourist interest, where foreign tourists could be attracted. The project was incurred totally by the central government. Part – II schemes included devilment of tourist facilities at places of interest of domestic tourist, which could also interest overseas visitors. On such projects, the central government met half the expenditure and the states met the rest. Part – III schemes included projects, which were primarily of domestic interest and were financed by the state governments. A number of tourist bungalows were constructed all over the country under the part-1 scheme now named 'Traveler's lodges". And some of them are still managed by the Indian tourism development corporation. Most accommodations built under part – I scheme were transferred to the states.

Central department of tourism completely took over the planning and development of facilities suitable for overseas tourists while the state government was assisted to develop facilities for domestic tourists state governments were free to shape their plans the way they liked. No matching subsides of fifty percent was given by the center. It was a good decision as the states started developing their own plans independently of central help through central guidance through the department of tourist and the planning commission was available. The new arrangement enabled the central department of tourism to expand its tourist promotion overseas by making available adequate quantity of better quality and variety of literature in a number of foreign languages.

The preamble to the fifth five-year plan for tourism explained the role of the center and the state governments. The center would undertake projects, which relate to the promotion of the international tourism and the states were advised to confine their projects to serve the needs of domestic tourists or budget tourist from overseas. The objectives laid down for the central department of tourism was the provision of accommodation and transport to match the anticipated growths in international tourism, to develop new resorts and tours to spread the traffic to different regions of the country.

For the first time in the sixth five-year plan, the planning commission recognized the importance of tourism in the following words.

Tourism, both domestic and international, had rapidly won considerable recognition as an activity generating a number of social and economic benefits like promotion of national integration and international understanding, creation of employment opportunities, removal of regional imbalances, augmentation of foreign exchange earnings, thus redressing the balance of payments situation.

The seventh plan (1985 – 1990) – focus on outdoor holidays

In the seventh year plan tourism received significant notice. Tourism related activities were given the status of an industry, which implied that such business activities would in future be entitled to the same incentives, and concessions as were applicable to the expert industry.

The eighth five-year plan underlines the fact that 15 states and 3 union territories had already declared tourism as industry-four more states had declared hotels as an industry. The plan recommended that other states might also accord similar priority to tourism.

The ninth plan 1997 – 2002 for tourism is ambitious – it envisages an expenditure of Rs.1000 crores 'Zone tourism development over the five – year period. Like the previous plan, the $9^{th}$ plan expects the government to act as a facilitator using the synergy of the private sector for developmental using tax concessions and other facilities as baits.

# TWO
# ORGANIZATION OF TOURISM

The term tourism refers to the activities of the visitor who travels to a certain geographical destination outside his or her usual surrounding of stay or work for not more than a year, for leisure, business or other purposes. They are not supposed to take up any remunerative assignment at the destination. Tourism is regarded as one of the fastest growing industries in the world. But it is not very well organised as it includes formal and informal sectors both. It is one of the most fragmented industries. But, to run any industry certain requirements are to be fulfilled. Industry needs an appropriate space; capital and infrastructure to bring the product in a usable form. It requires work force. Finally, when the product is out from the industry, there has to be a market for its consumption. All these are needed to fulfil the conditions of an industry. But tourism as an industry has some variations. The Policy of many governments in the world is considering it to be an industry. Hence, in this chapter, an attempt has been made to examine the concept, structure and components of tourism as an industry.

## 2.1 Tourism Organizations

INTERNATIONAL REGIONAL & NATIONAL TOURISM ORGANIZATIONS (updated November)

- Identify and classify different local and international tourism organizations
- Discuss each organization's function in the tourism industry
- Discuss the relationships of tourism organizations

## INTERNATIONAL CIVIL AVIATION ORGANIZATION

- Adapts international standards and to recommend practices for regulating air navigations.
- Encourage the improvement of the art of aircraft design and operation for peaceful purposes.

IATA or INTERNATIONAL AIR TRANSPORT ASSOCIATION

Aims to promote safe, regular and economical air transport, faster air commerce and study problems connected with the industry. Involves standardizing of tickets, prices, airline air way bills, baggage checks and other documents

WORLD TRAVEL & TOURISM COUNCIL

The only global forum whose members are the top decision makers in the travel and tourism industry. The 150 members are the CEO, President or Chairman of - airlines, airports, hotels, cruise lines, travel agencies, tour operators and travel technology suppliers The only body representing the private sector in all parts of the industry worldwide.

ORGANIZATION of ECONOMIC COOPERATION and DEVELOPMENT

Designed to achieve the highest sustainable economic growth and employment and raise standards of living of member countries Country Assistance Program Evaluation 26194 June 2008 Philippines Country Assistance Program Evaluation: Increasing Strategic Focus for Better Results

PATA or PACIFIC ASIA TRAVEL ASSOCIATION Develops, promotes and facilitates travel in the Pacific Areas Early leader in recognizing the need for environmental ethics Initiated the

PATA Code for Environmental Tourism CTA CTA or Caribbean Tourism Association/Organization Encourages and Assists in the development of tourism throughout the Caribbean Area.

## 2.2 IMPORTANCE OF TOURISM AS AN INDUSTRY

Source https://traveltractions.com/importance-of-tourism-types/

Tourism is one of the most labour-intensive industries of the world. It gives an employment opportunity to a large number of people all over the globe. It is considered as an industry, but it falls under the tertiary sector of economy. Traditionally speaking, industry is the one which transforms the raw material into finished goods and make the product more sustable for use. But in the tourism industry, a demarcation of the raw material and finished product is not clearly distinguishable. At one point of time, an input for tourism industry may be a finished product to be used by the tourists. For example, a tourist guide is the work force in the industry. They are the ones who guide the tourists and explain everything about the destination which is a great help for the tourists to know. But when the same guide is paid by the tourists for his services rendered to them, they become the end product of tourism industry. It is also a very important means to achieve the socio-economic development of a region. It helps in strengthening the economic condition of the region by providing livelihood to the local people in different ways. A large number of people are involved in the development of tourism. Those people may be with formal knowledge and training as well as from informal sector of the society. Tourism gives an opportunity even to the vendors, rickshaw pullers, auto-taxi drivers, apart from the highly qualified experts in hotel industry, IT and communication sector, long and medium haul transport, guides, ticketing, hotel booking, food and drinking etc. In the true sense, it is more of people involving service industry serving the need of the tourists. Providing livelihood to the people, it is able to remove many of the social and economic problems like poverty, under development and social discrimination. Tourism is also a medium through which global and regional socio-political harmony could be established. Its ability to generate socio-economic opportunities and help reducing the gap between rich and poor is more important than ever. Many advocators of tourism also consider that it is a "peace industry", a means to establish equilibrium of global peace process. Therefore, tourism developed and practised in a responsible and sustainable manner would bring peace and prosperity to the people of the tourists' destinations as well. At the regional and global level it would bring a geo-political stability.

## 2.3 COMPONENTS OF TOURISM INDUSTRY

Space for Tourism Industry Space is a basic component on which tourism occurs, as it is change of place from one area to another. The space for the tourism is almost the whole world.

Some parts of the world are more sought after while the others are not that important. It has region specific reasons. The availability of the required facilities for tourists makes the region resourceful. On the other hand, absence or qualitatively and quantitatively less availability of facilities makes the region less in demand by tourists. The facilities for tourists may be transport, hotels, hygienic food, accessibility, attractions etc. in that region. Safety and security is one of the very important aspects for tourism development. A region notorious for terrorism or politically unstable would definitely not attract many tourists. Therefore the growth and development of tourism depends on development of tourist products in that space

Entrepreneurship for Tourism Industry For an industry to be established there has to be someone who takes the responsibility to run the business. Since a large number of people wish to visit various places of tourists' interest, the entrepreneur takes the responsibility of providing facilities to the visiting tourists. In turn, they earn revenue along with the other local people. But many of the infrastructures are developed by the state government and not only by the individual/ organisations or institutions. Therefore, all of them are also accounted to be the entrepreneurs in the development of tourism.

Capital: Resource for Infrastructure Development A huge capital is needed to develop the infrastructure in any industry of a region. It is generally provided by the government under various policies. Thedevelopment of infrastructure is not confined only to the tourism industry, but it is for general well being of the area and people. The connectivity of the region with the rest of the country or the world, availability of regular electricity, hotels, good law and order condition, attractions for the tourists, good food facilities etc. are some of the requirements for tourists facilities. Many of them are facilitated by the government. Some of them are provided by different interested industrial institutions, organisations, entrepreneurs or hoteliers

Workforce for Tourism Industry There are many components of tourism over which its structure depends. Important among them are transport, accommodation, food, entertainment, hospitality, tourist attraction, tour operators, travel agents, and finally tourist etc. All of them are not separate entities but they exist in an interlinked manner. Their interaction is in the form of a web leading to finally serving the tourists. The tourism industry flourishes when qualified manpower is available to cater to the needs of the tourists. The manpower may be grouped into skilled, semiskilled as well as unskilled. All are required to meet the necessity of the tourists. For example, a highly skilled person is needed to book the tickets, take care of the hotel arrangement, and provide entertainment, guide and high-quality food. Local transport is provided by workforce like taxi driver and other helping staff. Making the tourists places neat, clean and tidy. Unskilled workforce is also needed and is utilised. The development of infrastructures is also associated with all kinds of workforce working together.

Market for Tourism Industry When do you think tourism flourishes?

The answer is when infrastructure is provided, accessibility is available, natural attractions are present, qualitative service providers are there, law and order is of utmost order, and people with spare time and money are in abundance; tourism is bound to flourish. Tourists are the consumers of services provided to them as per their wishes. Apart from the tangible items available, intangible services are also utilised by the tourists. The tangible items which physically exist like hotels, food, souvenir, taxies, guides, helpers etc. But the intangible services are completely different. It could be appreciated like the taste of food, peaceful environment, culture, entertainment, welcoming, sense of beauty etc. They are all used by tourists directly or indirectly. All of them are good reasons for the growth and development of the tourism industry in any particular region. Tourism marketing promotes the products developed to meet the needs of tourists. Generally, industries are those which produce similar goods and services and therefore, they are constantly in a state of competition. For example, productionof chips, cold drinks, ice creams, clothes, paper, cement, iron etc. are competing with each other in their categories. This sort of competition is not that strong, but they are complementary in nature in terms of providing products and services. An airline, hotel, travel agent may be competing in their categories, but all of them are supporting the tourism activities in that region. For tourism, they are harmonising the growth of tourism and that helps tourists. Their purpose is to provide the best services available and facilities to the tourists as per their requirements or choice. The input and output is not very explicitly separable in tourism industry. Other industries are defined by the product and services they produce with regard to the supply. With regard to tourism, it is driven by the demands of tourism. Other facilities are developed and provided in the region according to the demand of the tourists

## 2.4 SERVICES ASSOCIATED WITH TOURISM

There are many components of tourism. The main components of tourism may be put as producer, operator, travel agent and the tourists. All these are interconnected with tour operators and travel agents. The producer creates various resources which are needed for tourism. These resources could be put into both public and private sector. Now, let us briefly discuss them one by one. Overall there are various major components of tourism industry. They are

1. Accommodation
2. Food and Beverage
3. Travel trade
4. Transport
5. Attractions
6. Events and Conferences
7. Tourism services

### Accommodation

Accommodation is one of the fastest growing sectors of tourism industry. It plays a key role and it is a very basic component in industry. The demand of hotels exists almost throughout the year. Accommodations for the tourists are categorised on the basis of different methods like star rating, size, location, types of guests, alternative arrangements etc. The numbers are assigned on the basis of the facilities and services provided to the tourists/ guests. This classification is done by a central government committee known as Hotel Restaurant Approval Classification Committee (HRACC). One star hotel has the least facilities and services provided under the star category while the Five star has the maximum. Even, some seven star hotels are emerging up with the highest order of luxurious services. These facilities are of the highest order in terms of quality and space. Apart from the star ratings, some private budget hotels/guest houses are also providing accommodation facilities to the tourists under the economy category such as dormitory type and bed and breakfast. Classification on the basis of location: The location is also an important criterion to categorise the hotels. Some of them are very sought after becauseof the location, like many are situated near the airport, railway station or near the bus depot. Some hotels along the highways are also in demand as the tourists need them for stopovers or for overnight stay enroute. Under this category they may further be classified by business or commercial accommodation found mostly in big cities, business centers, tourist centers etc. Suburban accommodations are provided in the outskirts of cities and towns. In the same way accommodations are also available near the airports. Resorts and motels also cater to the need of the tourists in hilly areas or along the highways. Classification on the basis of the types of guests: Depending upon the facilities, space and privacy as well as the paying capacity of the guests, accommodations are grouped into commercial, suite, airport hotel, resort and motel. The first three accommodations are of the high order in terms of the rent of the rooms. A Suite is probably of the highest order having luxurious bed rooms apart from the living and dining room too. It serves the need of the rich categories of people like businessmen, film stars, politicians etc. Classification on the basis of supplementary/ alternate accommodation: Apart from the above mentioned categories, some other types of accommodations are also available. They are circuit houses, youth hostels, Yatri Niwas, forest lodges, Dak Bungalows and farm houses. A Circuit house is the tourist accommodation offering rooms to high ranking government officials. These are designed to offer good accommodations and food. Payment in cash is made on day basis and services provided. Youth hostels offers affordable rooms to young tourists. Yatri Niwas is a cheap accommodation normally found near beaches, lakes, railway stations, pilgrimage places etc. Forest lodge is for tourists who are visiting wildlife sanctuaries. Dak Bungalows are for the government servants who are on official visits.

**Food and Beverage**

Increase in the number of visiting tourists has led to an increase in the demand for food and beverage which has led to rise in their demand. This component of tourism is employing a great number of youths. The change is very apparent in the consumer preferences. It is leading to increasing competition; products are becoming sophisticated and specialised. Many restaurants are becoming specialised and creating a chain of their own. Their products are getting diversified. Food and beverage sector includes all sorts of consumption items used by the market forces. They are in immense demand and their outlets are coming up everywhere, at the roadside. In the hotels, lounges, dining rooms, coffee shops, fast food, pubs and bars

**Travel Trade**

Travel trade is concerned with the travelling of the tourists. It includes the selling/booking of reservation for travelling, accommodation, tours, transport, food and beverage etc. These bookings are done in two categories; all inclusive or at an individual basis. All inclusive tour booking is the one in which the tourists have to pay an amount fixed or negotiated, between the tour operators and the tourists. Generally, the tour operators fix the rate depending upon the size of the tourists group and duration. They even go for negotiation to reduce the charge. Booking for the individual or group of individuals for a sector of tourism is more of a fixed rate by the tour operator. It may include booking of reservations for travelling, accommodation, tours, transport, food and beverage etc. It is known as retail travel operation. All inclusive packages take care of everything associated with travel, like accommodation, site seeing, food, entertainment etc. This group of tour operation is sometimes known as wholesale tour operation

**Transport**

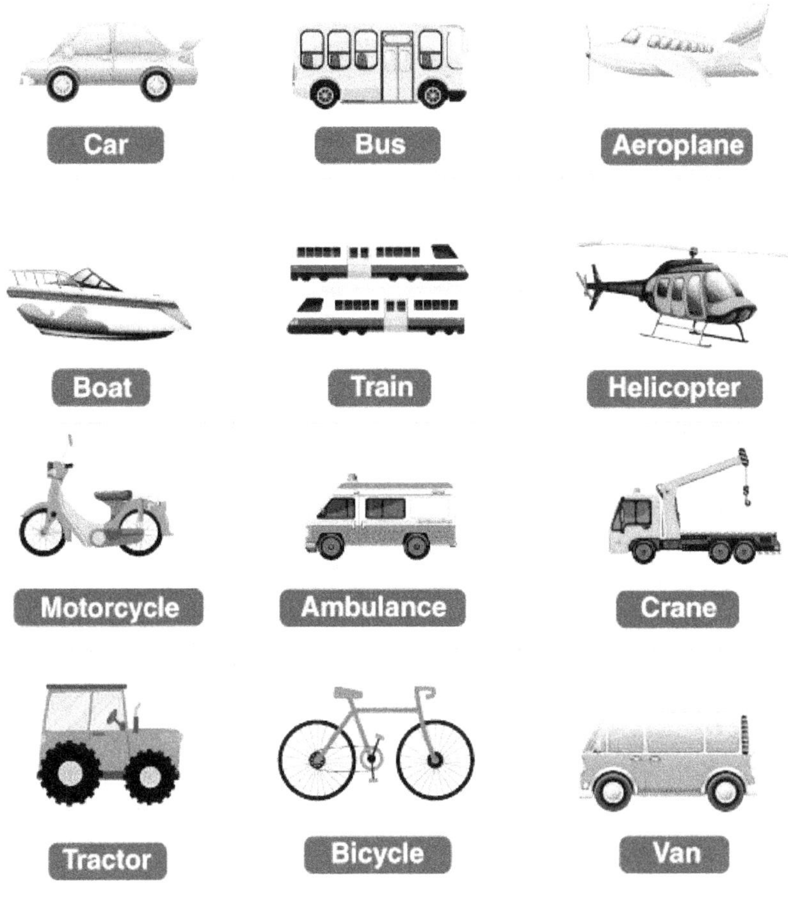


Source = https://byjus.com/english/transport-names/

Transport is one of the essential components of tourism activities. The relationship between transport and tourism development has traditionally been regarded as 'chicken and egg'. Transport contributes significantly in fulfilling the social and economic development of the area concerned. It overcomes the physical constrains of distance and meet the human needs for movement over the space. It provides a link between origin of tourism and its destination. Human movement at national and international level is taking place because of various means of transport. Millions of tourists expect to be transported safely, quickly and comfortably to their destinations at a reasonable cost. In fact, transport and its associated infrastructure have facilitated the human mobility on a large scale with lesser problems. Transport sector is divided into four types. They are air, rail, road and water transport which has different characteristics and advantages over the other. All of them are catering to the need of economically different categories of travellers and tourists. A brief description of each of them is given below: Railways: The railway provides a great advantage of travelling for a long distance in a country or a group of countries where this facility is available. It is a cheap mode of transport and serves every category of travellers. Huge number of people can travel together. If the distance is long, the railway is a convenient mode of transport in comparison to road. It is faster and safer than road. Special trains have been introduced for tourists in India. It provides all sorts of facilities on the wheel. The details about the railways transport and its characteristics can be read from this internet source

**Airways**: Airways is very important for foreign tourists as many of the countries are not linked with rail or road transport. It is the fastest means of transport but it is costly. Many of the countries are connected by air and it reduces the distance. Air transport has accelerated tourism in a big way, particularly the international tourism

**Roadways**: Road provides a door to door transport service and connects all the transport systems combining them together. It has given access to the destinations for tourists. Air transport has brought the world to the door steps but road transport has connected all the utility rooms inside the door. Theimportance and the characteristics of road transport can be seen in Lesson 5 on Transport for Tourism. In fact it takes the tourist right upto the monument, place of worship or to the house of the host.

**Waterways**: Waterways include ferry, cruise, water taxis and other forms of water transport. They may be of the open seas or inland transport as well. Water transport was very popular before the advent of motorised vehicles. In the olden days, the water was considered an important means of transport. Because of the increased importance of road, rail and air, the services of water transport taken by passengers has gone down drastically. The details of the water transport can be seen in the following source

### Events and Conferences

Many academic, professional, business or government events, meetings and conferences are organised. They deliberate on the topics chosen for the events. They invite the people from various parts of the world. They are supposed to travel to the places of the event and its surroundings. At that place, accommodation and food are essentially required for them. They are offered entertainment. All these involve spending on the part of tourist. They manage the money from their own pockets or get sponsorships. Sometimes the organisations bear the cost where they are working. Some of the delegates are also financially helped by the organisers. The organisers themselves get the financial supports from the government, ministries, business houses, academic institutions etc. Conferences, seminars, meetings, trade shows, exhibitions and conventions are big business for many communities. Because of these types of events local people earn by providing and selling tourist services and products. When people arrive at such places, they visit the nearby areas. Therefore, most cities of the world organise many meetings and conferences from time to time, especially at destinations which are places of tourist interest like Goa, Delhi, Mumbai, Kolkata' besides many other places like Pragati Maidan at Delhi is booked almost the whole year for events at national or international level. The same is the case of other cities and towns in India and abroad.

**Tourism Services**

The sector of tourism services includes many organisations, associations, government agencies, companies etc. All of them have specialised services which the tourism industry needs. They are basically a sort of regulators which provide services. They fullfil not only the need of the travellers and tourists but also serve the purpose of growth and development in a specific region. Hence, conducting a research becomes an important component for tourism. Apart from research in tourism; advertising, marketing, educating/informing about tourism are other good components of the tourism industry. The government plays an important role in providing basic infrastructures so that tourism is well developed and organised. It encourages business by providing money, information and services. In this process the government conducts market research for finding out industry demands, problems andprofiles of tourists at different intervals of time. It is a very important tool in assisting the marketing planning and management of services and facilities provided to tourists. Their demand in tourism is assessed and finally a decision is taken, which helps in the growth of tourism. For all these, a proper and balanced plan and policy are needed for which the government is the right authority to take a decision. One can find dozens of advertisements about tourism in the newspaper everyday, inviting tourist to their destinations. For example honeymoon trip, pilgrimage trip, cruise trip, mountaineering, rafting, national site visit, international visit; All these are working together for the promotion of tourism as well as getting financial benefits out of them

## 2.5 RECENT TRENDS IN TOURISM

**5 LATEST TRENDS IN HOSPITALITY**

**1. Minimalism & Natural Design**
Less clutter and simple interiors

**5. Personalisation for Loyal Guests**
Special service for returning guests

**2. Sustainability & Eco Tourism**
Add plants and use sustainable decor

**4. Smart Technology**
Use artificial intelligence

**3. Healthy Food & Beverage**
Include vegan, organic, gluten free meals

Source - https://blog.staah.com/tips-trends/5-easy-ways-to-make-sure-you-are-following-these-latest-trends-in-hospitality

National policies for the development and promotion of tourism in India are designed by the Union Ministry of Tourism in consultation and collaboration with other Central Ministries, State Governments, Union Territories and representatives of the private sector. Special efforts are being made to explore new forms of tourism and promote the existing tourism along with the latest trends such as stay on houseboat, stay in villages for a feel of the countryside location. The other trends being cruise, medical, business, sports and eco tourism etc. Since the beginning of the mid-20th century there has been an immense growth of tourism in the world. The growth of arrivals of tourists in East Asia and the pacific is very strong. New unknown destinations are coming in a big way and showing higher growth. Europe and America were the main tourists destination before 2000, but recently their share has declined by 10% and 13%, respectively

At present, travel for leisure, recreation and holidays constitutes about 51% of the international tourist arrivals. Approximately 15% of the tourists are taking the journey for business and professional purposes. The other 27% travel for visiting friends and relatives, religious pilgrimages and for medical tourism. The remaining 7% of the visitors are taking up their journey for not any specific purposes as per the record of the data. About 52% of the total tourists travel by 38% by road, 3% by train and remaining 6% by water transport. The details of the world trend of tourism may be read in the next chapter. The World Tourism Organisation has projected that international arrivals would reach nearly 1.6 billion by 2020. Out of this, 1.2 billion would be expected to be intra-regional and 0.4 billion would be long distance travellers. East Asia and the Pacific, south Asia, Middle East and Africa are expected to grow more than 5% per year, while the world average would be 4.1%. More mature regions such as Europe and America are anticipated to show lower than average growth rate. The total tourist arrivals shows that by 2020 top three destinations would be Europe (717 million), East Asia (397) and the America (282 million), followed by Africa, the Middle East and South Asia.

**Recent Trends of Tourism in India**

India is one of the favoured destinations of foreign tourists. From 2009 to 2011, the foreign tourist arrivals have increased tremendously from all regions of the world. In 2011, the foreign tourist arrival in India from Eastern Europe is 20.6%, followed by South East Asia (18.8%), West Asia (18.5%), East Asia (15.5%), Africa (13.6%), Australasia (10.9%), South Asia (8.8%), North America (5.6%) and Western Europe (5.0). It is because India has great variety of tourist places as well as attractions, discussed in this lesson. It is also a reality that India is very economical destination. This may be seen in terms of general tourism as well as for medical tourism. That is why, the stay in India is not very costly and, hence, the foreign tourists prefer to stay for longer duration. As per the available data, the stay of foreign tourist in India is the highest, a little more than a month (31.2 days) on an average. It is followed by Australia (27 days), Pakistan (25 days). The details of recent trends of tourism in India may be read in proceeding chapters.

## 2.6 ROLE OF THE GOVERNMENT OF INDIA IN POPULARIZING TOURISM

The ministry of Tourism is the nodal agency for the formation of national policies and programmes and for the coordination of activities of various Central Government Agencies, State Governments/UTs and the private sectors for the development and promotion of tourism in India. This Ministry is headed by the Union Minister of State of Tourism (Independent Charge). The administrativehead of the Ministry is the Secretary (Tourism) who also acts as the Director General (DG) Tourism. The Directorate General of Tourism has a field formation of 20 offices within the country and 14 offices abroad and one project i.e. Indian Institute of Skiing and Mountaineering (IISM)/Gulmarg Winter Sport Project. The Union Ministry of Tourism has under its charge a public sector undertaking, the India Tourism Development Corporation (ITDC) and the following autonomous institutions. z India Institute of Tourism and Travel Management (IITTM) and National Institute of Water Sports (NIWS) z National Council for Hotel Management and Catering Technology (NCHMCT) and the Institutes of Hotel Management.

**Role and Functions of the Ministry of Tourism**

- All policy matters including development, incentives, external assistance, promotion and marketing etc.
- Planning and coordination with other Ministries, Departments, States/UTs
- Human Resource Development
- Publicity and Marketing
- Research, analysis, monitoring and evaluation
- Legislation and Parliamentary Work
- Vigilance matters
- Approval and classification of hotels and restaurants
- Approval of travel agents, inbound tour operators and tourist transport operators, etc.

Tourism infrastructure development for quality tourism is the key area of this ministry More than 50% of the Ministry's expenditure is incurred for the development of tourism at various tourist destinations and circuits in the States/UTs. Keeping in view the professional work force requirements of the country's fast expanding accommodation and catering industry, the Ministry of Tourism reoriented and remodelled various training programmes in order to harness the resources and also to provide a central thrust to the Tourism industry. So, in the year 1982, Union Ministry of Tourism established the National Council for Hotel Management and Catering Technology (NCHMCT). With the vast expansion and modernisation of the country's hospitality industry, hotel management and catering, educational programme have gained tremendous

# THREE

## Functions of Modern Travel Agency

## 3.1 TOUR OPERATORS

# TYPES OF TOUR OPERATORS

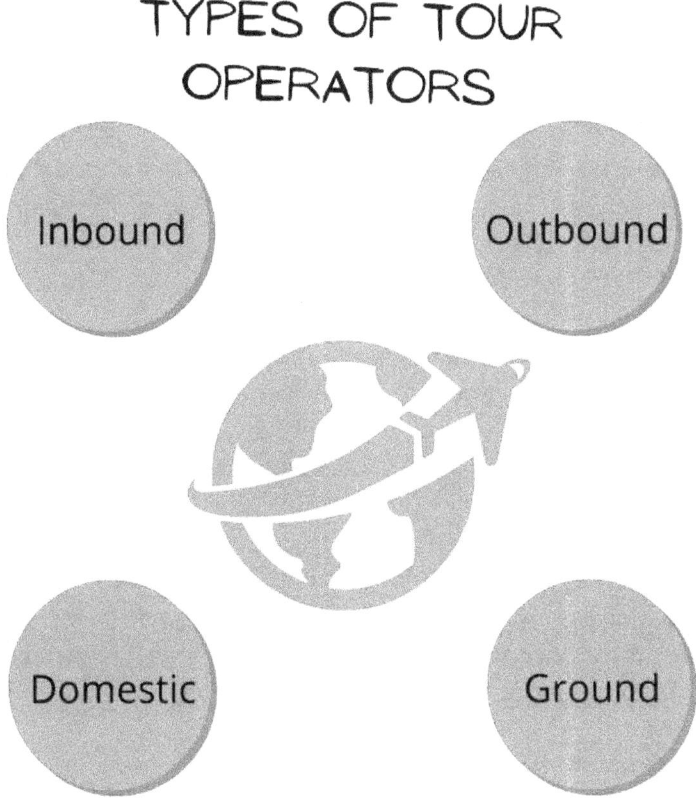


Source -https://blogs.travstack.com/blog/difference-between-tour-operator-and-travel-agent-392166

In west Asia, national tourist organisations do exist in one form or another. However, with the exception of Israel and Jordan, others are not involved in serious tourism promotion. Iran was active before the revolution but it has since changed its concept of tourism. The industrial revolution was a long time in coming to Asia where most countries were directly or indirectly under colonial rule.

Tourism development in this region was different from Europe because inspiration direction and guidance for development came from the government and not from for people. Some Asian government offered a variety of loans and incentives for quicker development of tourist infrastructure like hotels and transport. Governments also organized and subsidized training programmes for the manpower needed by this industry.

The overseas tourist office formed an extension of the national tourist originations and directly approached travelers and tour operators selling tourist destinations. Today, all major countries and even small states, districts etc. have national tourist organisations often charged with the development of infrastructure for tourism at home and marketing of their tourist product overseas.

## 3.2 FUNCTIONS OF TOUR OPERATORS:

### Meaning:

Tour operator is one who buys the individual elements in the travel product on his own account and combines them in such a way that he is selling a package travel, the tour, to his clients. He is remunerated by a reasonable mark up on the prices he had paid the providers of the services, which make up the package. The tour operator is a manufacturer of a particular travel product.

Tour operators play an important part in the promotion of tourism. The main function is to get tourists from abroad and make necessary arrangements for their accommodation, transport, sight-seeing all over the country according to the individual requirements of the tourists.

### Functions:

A major contributing factor in this grown of air travel holiday tourism has been the development of the inclusive tour, a method of packaging a holiday. Essentially and inclusive tour is a package of transport and accommodation and perhaps some other services, which is sold as a single holiday for an all-inclusive price.

The tour operator who buys aircraft seats and hotel beds and certain other facilities such as surface transports or entertainment and makes up the package, tour operator makes all the necessary arrangements-transport, accommodation, sight-seeing insurance, entertainment and other matters and sells this 'package' for an all inclusive price.

Exerting an active influence on the supplier of services and in order to ensure that the services supplied are first rate and meet the normal requirement of tourist traffice.

In guiding tourist traffic towards tourist areas, besides ensuring air/rail/ sea reservation for travel, he has obtain hotel reservations, confirmation for onward journey and also obtaining passport, p' form liquor permits, customs clearance, visas, foreign currency, travelers cheques and similar other matters and also to supply literature on the places to be visited and give miscellaneous advice on any subjects as demanded by his clients.

They produce attractive brochure and carry the burden of most of the publicity, promotion and marketing services, for the principal or manufacture of services.

Tour operator's business has two departments as far as tourism a concerned. They have a department for the outgoing traffic and they have department for the incoming traffic.

The tour operator would have to include Sales, Research and Planning. Finance and Accounts, destination and service and Publicity and Public Relations, possession of Professional knowledge and experience, as for instance, schedules of train connections. Rate of hotels, their quality, whether rooms have baths, etc.

### 3.3 Types of Tours

Tourism is of two types domestic or internal and foreign or international

**Domestic Tours:**

in all the touristically advanced countries, domestic tourism occupies a predominant place in the overall picture of tourist traffic in domestic tourism, people travel from their normal domicile to other areas in their own country.

They find this travel easy and convenient as the same language and currency is used in the country, no documentation, passports or visas are required. Domestic tourism does not involve any balance of payment.

Domestic is full of economic social and cultural benefits home tourism is the key to national integration. The function of domestic tourism is to foster a sense of unity and an appreciation of regional diversity, and awareness of understanding of their countries past and of her more recent as well as ancient history.

The domestic tourism in the country was limited to two extremes pilgrimage by third class trains, of travel by first class trains or travel by rich people to hill stations who never travel in groups.

### *Distinction between domestic and foreign tourism:*

1. In economic term, domestic tourism stands on a different footing from foreign tourism.
2. Earning from domestic tourism cannot claim any extra weightage in investment planning.

3. Earning from foreign tourism in the form of foreign exchange claim extra weightage in investment planning.
4. Demand for domestic can easily be regulated
5. It is not possible or regulate the demand for foreign tourism.
6. The demand for domestic tourism reflects the inter national distribution of incomes.
7. It does not reflect the international distribution of income

**Foreign Tourism**

When people travel to a country other than their own with a different economic and political system, the movement becomes foreign tourism. It involves preparation of various documents to cross the frontiers and conversion of currency.

These difficulties are gradually diminishing as documentation is becoming increasingly less. Visas are being abolished or relaxed and some of the countries are forming currency and customs unions. We are slowly moving towards free movement of people.

Individual and group travel, the tourist moves about individually or as a member of a group, irrespective of the way travel or stay is arranged. It is further classified into (a) independent travel, and (b) inclusive travel or tours. In the case of independent, tour, transport, accommodation and other element of travel are arranged separately either by the tourist himself or by his travel agent. The technical word for such a traveler is FIT- free independent traveler. As a member of the inclusive group, the tourist buys a trip, for which he is unable to distinguish the prepaid cost of his fare, accommodation and other elements. Inclusive tours are also called package tours.

Another term-mass tourism-refers to the participation of a large number of people in tourism.

**3.4 Tour Brochures:**

Reference has earlier been made to the preparation of an itinerary, its contents and the regulation regarding code numbers, maps or illustrations and minimum quantity requirements of tour literature. It has also been started that a tour brochure or folder is an important means to inform, influence and induce customers to buy the tours offered by tour operators, travel agents or carriers. A brochure must, therefore, fulfill its functions, bearing in mind that in the highly completive field of tour packaging, large numbers of brochures are produced and distributed. It is obligatory to have good quality brochures which are attractive informative, have a stamp of creativity and are languaged in good copy, are varnished with colourful maps of photographs which would dignify the tour and be readily acceptable to discerning customers.

The brochure must be distinctive and delineate the objective of a tour and adequately describe the tour, the service or areas its attractions and give all the required information to its readers and details of what a customer may expect. Badly conceived and poorly produced brochures, with an indifferent copy and splashed with popular adjectives which appear with constant frequency mean little to the general public and are a dead loss, it is advisable to avoid matter which is misleading, has overstatements and exaggerations. A good quality folder must be up-to-date in information and dead literature should be discarded quickly. Production of brochures and other travel literatures is expensive and in order for these to be effective they should be professionally created and produced by experts in the line.

We must now allude to the basic requirement of a tour brochure and its contents.

a. firstly, the design layout, copy, illustrations, size, quality of paper, quantity, printing, budget and other production details have to be settled and these would be influenced by the intention to have a single itinerary, brochure or a general brochure incorporating many itineraries like visits to different countries or areas or it is is intended to produce a special interest tour brochure, offering itineraries say, for a gardens tour, a Buddhist monument or temples tour, etc. in each case, the design, approach and other production components would be different and care has to be taken to produce distinctive brochures which attract and satisfy the readers. The brochure is generally folder type with a cover. Operators may, however, produce shells for use in special areas or for special interest tours, with standard conditions printed on the shell. Filler sheets covering itineraries may be attached to the shell to make up a brochure and where amendments take place frequently, this may be the most economical way of brining out up-to-date brochures.

a. The cover of brochure or the front page of a shell would normally indicate the following:

    i. Type and name of tour e.g. destination of tour, to Asia or Europe or far East etc.. or, as stated above, special interest tours. Descriptive or sometimes fanciful names are given to the tours depending upon what is being offered.

    ii. An attractive photograph or illustration depicting or tied-in within the theme of the tour.

    iii. Name of tour operator or carrier promoting the tour (contact address may be given inside)

    iv. Carriers to be used

    v. Departure dates for tours and the number of days of the tour, if a single tour.

c. The complete itinerary would be printed inside, giving departures, arrivals carriers hotels designated, brief description of sight seeing arrangements, visits to places and countries, showing where and when the tour begins, goes to and ends. A brochure may include a single tour or many tours; in the later case, complete itineraries of each side-tour must be given separately and identifiably Each itinerary would have an IT code number, a route map, the price of the tour and the number of days of a tour, the dates for which the tour would be operated, whether escorted or unescorted. Optional and side-tour may be clearly indicated and cost differentials specified.

d. A tour brochure should be a complete and self-sufficient document, giving the essential information that a prospective traveler may require.

**Guidelines:**

Let us now discuss how tours could be sold successfully and what guidelines may be worthwhile in this behalf. Basically, the general principles of marking and sales promotion would be applicable and these have to borne in mind. However, a few pertinent points call for special attention so that the high mortality rate of tours can be brought down:

2. Tours must be planned and packaged after market research reveals what tours are and would be in demand be in demand, historic trends are also a good indicator. Including tours with no potential for success and merely to pad the brochure is not a good policy.

4. Create new tours, introduce lesser know areas and offer new interests and make them attractive. Be a leader, an innovator and an expert; but this calls for careful evaluation of all factors, proper planning and hard work. Do not pact too many places and too much into your tours.

5. Ensure a right price for the tour and services offered. It must be good value for the tour to be successful.

6. Tour offerings must be made at proper time, and tours have own time, place and season to promote depending upon the habits of customers, their patterns and the type of a tour. National traits show that the English plan their next holidays around December , the Germans even as late as February the French still later, while the Americans more that six months in advance. Select the best dates and season, during which to concentrate on a coordinated group of offerings and provide a good selection for the customers.

7. the tour promoter must familarise himself fully with components of each tour, the services and attractions offered and must personally and critically experience what the tour has to offer. he must personally know to the contractors, their competence and examine the equipment to the used by them and have a full awareness of quality and reputation of the personal who deals with the tour groups.

8. By the time the tour is offered all carrier reservation ground transfer arrangement and sightseeing agreements must be firmly concluded and no loose ends left united.

9. Familiarize with the market segments having potential for sales of the tours the tour operator must act with personal knowledge, perspicacity enthusiasm and purposefulness to reach and influence his customers.

10. a) prepare a carefully conceived and professionally formulated marketing plan and follow it scrupulously and vigorously

b) Make use of newsletters brochures for a mailing compaign and slides, films show cards, displays and other visual aids in publicising and selling the tours.

c) Prepare effective hard hitting and imaginative presentation and make these amongst community groups, the clubs, associations and educational institutions on a pre-planned basis.

d) Use trade magazines, special interest journals and general press selectively and with telling effect.

e) Arrange special presentation for travel agents with detailed, information on tariffs, bulk sales, commissions, sales aids procedures for effecting reservations, cancellations, extensions of tours. Etc., suggest to agents promotional activities, which would stimulate client motivation for interest in these tours. Also, inform them what promotional material is available to provide support for the tours to be sold by them. Ensure that adequate copies of brochures with tariffs are supplied to the agents.

9.  obtain sales deads, information about prosespects and indicated interest of old customers and follow up all these leads effectively to sell the tours.

10.  Experience shows that it takes a minimum of six months to promote and sell a tour. Review progress of the compaign from time to time and make changes in marketing strategy, if necessary or consider deviations extensions. Etc. for better results.

11.  Critically analyses response to tour offerings, eliminate tours doubtful of success and pursue those in demand. Cash in on the popularity of tour.

12.  Cut mortality rate of tours, firmly establish reasons for such mortality and essess the cost.

13.  Release transportation space, booked or blocked with carriers and adjust ground arrangements consequent upon elimination of tours or reduction of size of tour groups send final confirmations. To ground contractors at his earliest.

14.  Keep close contact with tour progress, and ensure avoidance of complaints at all stages. Secure feedback from tour customers on tours completed, for more satisfactory operations in future.

15.  Do not repeat your mistakes and learn from the past.

With the examination in detail of the structure and components of a tour, packaging and marketing tours successfully should not be found too difficult by these interest in this business.

## 3.5 ROLE OF COMMUNICATION IN TRAVEL

In the field of travel and tourism, communication plays a very crucial role as it is through this that a potential customer obtains information about a produce which in the final analysis is a destination which he proposes to visit. Travel being a service industry the need for not only accurate but rapid information about a destination becomes paramount for the satisfaction of the consumer. The importance of communication in various fields including travel and tourism has been well recognized. World renowned space scientist, Arthur C.Clarke, addressing the first meeting of the inter-government council of the international programme of the Development of Communication held in Paris in the year 1981, said, "In many ways and for many purposes, printed matter, books, newspapers and wallpapers will always be the best and the cheapest form of communication. But now electronics have given us tools that can perform miracles impossible to the printed word and which, of course, can reach millions who are unable to read. The newest and most powerful of these communication devices depend upon space technology, a fact that s not generally recognized"

In the period between 1981 (When Arthur Clarke spoke about the newest and most powerful communication devices) and today, with a gap of fifteen years, there has been virtually a revolution in the various techniques in the field of communication and information. The various charges that have taken place since then have greatly benefited everyone. The electronics have performed such miracles in the last two decades that today we find ourselves in the middle of a new world, a world of information revolution.

The development have greatly facilitated rational management of the business world. Newer techniques of data processing mainly transmission of data and techniques of data and telecommunication, have already formed a new field of activity, characterized by an enormous potential for growth and development telecommunication devices are in use today in almost all fields of economy.

The new means of public telecommunication systems as tele-text, telecopy or videotext have given a very tough competition to earlier pioneer public communication means such as newspapers, magazines, etc. However, the new means of communication also offer great possibilities for improvement, rationalization and the expansion of the existing facilities data collection and transmission. Today the mass media world over has immensely benefited from the new technology and information techniques.

## 3.6 MODERN MASS MEDIA TECHNIQUES

Understanding of the modern mass media techniques as also the mass media means are necessary for a person working in the travel and tourism field as knowledge of these will help in keeping with fast changing scenario in the business of travel the modern mass media techniques can be grouped as under.

a.  Satellite television
b.  Cable television networks

c.  Video text
d.  Internet

All the four modern mass media techniques are widespread in the world and are considered to be crucial for business and industry. Their mass media techniques however have some limitations as far as their used for a specific person or an individual is concerned. Because of their widespread coverage and their technical methods of transmission these cannot be directed for the used of a specific person. Besides, the receiver of the information through these techniques cannot start a dialogue or communicate with another person the communication, therefore is limited to one way.

For the direct transmission of information, there are different modern means which have been developed and are quite widespread . the inter flow of information through these means is possible these means are as follows.

a.  Teletex
b.  Telecopy
c.  Telebox
d.  Videobox
e.  Telefax
f.  E-mail

**Teletex**
Teletex is an improvement over teletex and has in fact developed from it. The receiver for teletex is an electronic "typewrite", which can send electronically enriched "letters" to owners of ordinary telex equipment- the transmission of message time is usually shorter in comparison with time taken with telex. Besides, it is also possible to transmit more office typewriter symbols. A normal electronic typewriter can be used as a receiver for teletex.

**Telecopy**
Telecopy provides the possibility of exchanging photocopies through a date network, information in the form of either written document or technical drawing is remote copied. This means that two facilities for copying are connected, one at the sender's end and the other at the receiver's end. Transmission time is only a few minutes.

**Videotex**

Videotex occupied a special position among the "new media". It plays a key role in the link between telecommunication and the computer sciences. Its advantages lie in the possibility it provides for linking computers, and also in its interactive dialogue capabilities. Using a videotext, information and communication systems can be converted into interactive systems capable of communicating with one another. In fact, the videotex is a multipurpose instrument with multiplicity of uses. It serves as:

a.  An instrument for data processing
b.  An information medium:
c.  A communication system; and
d.  A marketing instrument

This relatively new service connects various forms of use of the above mentioned facilities and at the same time offers some other possibilities. To operate the services, a television set with a decoder and telephone is necessary without which the service cannot operate. In Europe, nearly all households have television sets and a telephone and with the help of video-tex separate households can be reached in large area. Members of German BTX service as well as members of France Telecom service can now obtain all kinds of information from external computers or use data bank, all through their television sets. In many other countries in Europe, USA etc. similar systems are in use.

The use of videotext (VTX) is prevalent today in many fields. In addition to its use in the field of business as it allows fast message transmission, fast and inexpensive data collection and upto data information which are crucial for advertising, the system is also used by specialized groups of users for collecting orders in field. It is also used in the field of tourism as a one way system, for extensively (VTX) is the most advantageous means of communication, taking into account its low cost and the wider range of its application.

**Telebox**

Telebox is an electronic post office box system, Each member of the system has his or her "post offices Box" in the computer, where other members can leave their message the owner of each box can electrically contact the others.

## 3.7 COMPUTER TECHNOLOTY IN TOURISM

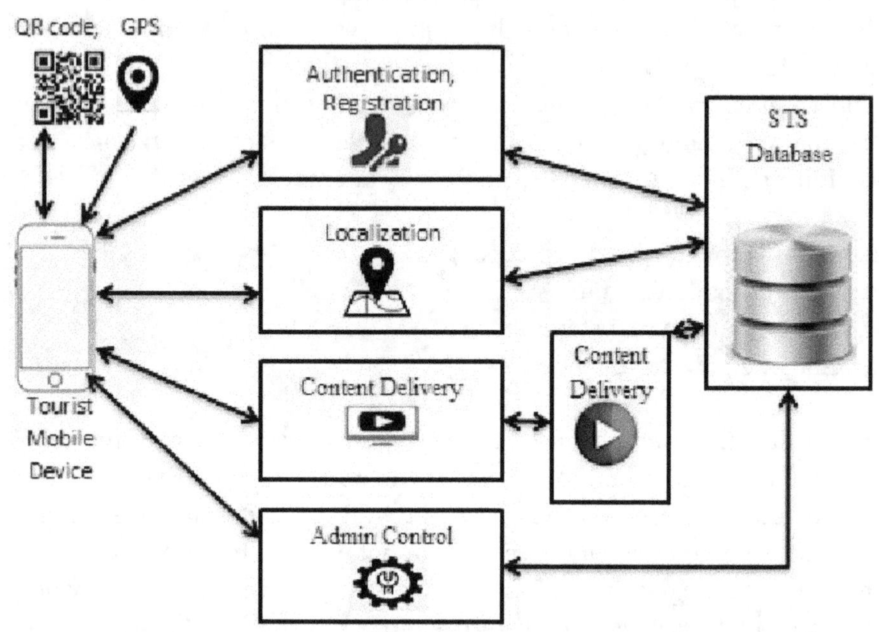


Entehttps://www.semanticscholar.org/paper/Smart-Tourism-
Architectural

In the field of tourism, the computer has made entry in a big way. A computer is a managerial tool capable of processing large volumes of data rapidly. It can perform basic arithmetic functions (addition subtraction, division and multiplication) and logical operations (strong ranking and assembling) in a fraction of a second. A computer dispenses result in a large variety of formats, these are capable of repeating programmed instruction almost endlessly without an error, and maintaining a vast data base of stored information for possible future use. Today a computer can be but to variety of uses in the day to day activities.

Although the computer were in use in some way or other in various branches of tourism industry since the early sixties, today these are considered as indispensable these are extensively used in almost all branches of the travel industry. They are part and parcel of a travel agency and are playing a key role in making the task of providing travel services an easy affair computers lately are undertaking among other job, the planning of vacation s for an individual and his family through home terminals the principle users of computers in the travel industry are.

1. Airline companies
2. Hotel companies
3. Railways
4. Shipping & Cruise Lines
5. Travel agents
6. Tour Operators

### 3.8 USE OF COMPUTERS BY AIRLINES

Today almost al the airlines use computers for their entire reservation work. The sudden growth about thirty-five years ago in the global travel put a big pressure on the handling of air traffic, especially the passenger traffic had begun to indicate that handling reservation manually could not sustained long without effecting efficiency in the customer service. It was then that a need to computerized passenger reservation systems was felt by the major airlines of the world.

IBM took the initiative and developed a computerized reservation system known as programmed Airlines Reservation System (PARS) this system was developed in the early 1960s. However, PARS was not developed exclusively for or with any one particular airline. The system was designed as an all purpose software package that would fit the requirements of any domestic airline, it was designed around IBM's new hardware range system 360, which was subsequently to revolutionise the entire computer industry.

The first airline to use PARS was the United States based continental airlines in the year 1967. this was followed by most major US airlines which used the system making PARS the most popular and successful software product of the time this was a major achievement for IBM. the system later expanded to meet the needs of several other airlines outside the United States of America resulting in the creation of international programmed Airlines Reservation System (IPARS). Initially this system was a joint venture between IBM and British Overseas Airways Corporation (BOAC) and aimed at adapting PARS to the needs of airlines that had mainly international operations.

Subsequently, many airlines adopted the system. The international package became almost as much of a standard as PARS, although many airlines modified the system extensively, IPARS was at the base of most international airlines system. By the late 1960s, the system developed was known as CPARS (C for Compacto this system was flowed by a system known as Univac

Standard Airline System, USA with the passing of the years more and more system developed, incorporating more functions to enable the airlines to have more transactions and instructions. The functions of various system are basically identical across all airline reservation systems. The differences between them are in areas no apparent to the passengers, such as the flexibility with they can handle control of space of lights, particularly where multiple classes and multiple sectors are involved.

The popularity of any system to a large extent depends on its coverage and online reservation network. The number of terminals which a system has is also an important consideration . the more the terminals a system has, the larger will be the online reservation network the number of reservation transactions carried out by a system in a given time is another important aspect. However, it became obvious that the system was too costly, for smaller international airlines developed their own IBM oriented reservation system in the early 1970 s to be considered main aspects are important to make a system perfect and universally acceptable.

1. number of reservation transaction to be handled,
2. data link with other airlines
3. number of terminals
4. information processing capacity, and
5. data volume capacity.

In recent years a major advance has been made in the airline reservation system in Germany a computer system capable of carrying out as many as 1,000 reservation transactions every second, involving data links with 28 airlines, a host of car hire agencies and hotels and about 20-000 travel agencies in Europe alone has been set up at Erding in the southern part of Germany the system, knows as "Amadeus" has been developed jointly at a cost of dm 350 million by four airlines – Air France Iberia, SAS and Lufthansa. The information processing capacity of the mainframe IBM and Unisys computers installed at Erding the world's largest computer centre, involves a data volume equivalent to a library of 3,50,000 books.

**Computers in Air Cargo**

Most of the airlines are now using computers for cargo handing operations as well the handling of cargo shipments on ground is a costly affair and the cost has been increasing over the years. Almost 50 percent of the handling of cargo shipment reflect the cost of manual information processing. Freight rate increases have not kept pace with cost increase, so airlines had either to accept reduced margins or take steps to reduce costs as this speeds up the hoarding of information related to consignments and also reduces the time the cargo spends on the ground the pioneer in cargo computerization was Alitalia whose o4-cargo system was adopted and modified by many major airlines such as Swiss-air, TWA and British Airways Univac's USAS has a fully developed cargo module almost all the major airlines in the world have now adopted one or another system of cargo computerization.

**Advantage to travel agents**

Today several airlines have developed and adopted sophisticated computer systems for their use the airlines also make available their system to their appointed sales agents, the sale agents are equipped with an appropriate terminal and receive the necessary instruction and procedures. Airlines have thus greatly benefited from the use and adaptation of computers some of the major advantages of use of computes.

By airlines include.

A.  High profile applications like passenger reservations
B.  Applications of departure, control and cargo
C.  Accounting, budgeting forecasting and planning
D.  engineering management
E.  cargo management
F.  revenue accounting
G.  fare quotations and construction;
H.  ticket printing
A.  crew scheduling
J.  crew management, and
K.  yield optimisation

## 3.9 ROLE OF COMPUTER IN RESERVATIONS

The role of SITA, societe international de tele communications Aeronautiques in airlines automation has been very crucial automation is the key to achieving a higher level of productivity in any industry, especially in the airlines industry, and automation of airline functions will continue with more emphasis being put towards achieving short-tem benefits

SITA is responsible for providing Data Processing Services in fact, it is the major supplier of information handling services for the airlines industry. Its aims are to foster efficient telecommunications, date processing and transmission means for all categories of information required in the operation of air transport enterprises with the specific aim of promoting safe and regular air transport in all countries.

There has always been a continued high growth of demand for the services offered by SITA it provides data processing services in the following areas:

I. Passenger Reservations
II. Departure control
III. Meteorological data
IV. Credit authorization and Document Verification
V. Baggage tracing (BAGTRAC)
VI. Share cargo services
VII. Share flight operations date base
VIII. Flight planning
IX. Baggage Handling management services
X. Common customs interface system
XI. Fuel management
XII. Airline schedules and flight Availability data base
XIII. IATA passenger Tariff Conference Support
XIV. SITA is providing a valuable service to the airlines. Almost all the information required in the operation of air transport in the world is being provided to the airlines industry. The range of services offered by SITA is very extensive and new services are being added as and when these are required.

### 3.10 COMPUTER IN RAILWAY

in addition to use of computer by airlines retail agents, travel agents and tour operators, these are also being used directly by the railway systems.

The railway system in Europe and some other countries have now been using computers extensively. In countries like France. Germany, Switzerland and Belgium, to name a few, computers have been in use for over a decade. The most important use of computers in railways however is in the area of ticket reservation. The information regarding availability of seats is now available instantly in various networks. Railway system now use the computers for route planning, engineering accounting inventory planning and control, purchase and a host of other functions.

The most remarkable use of computer in railways has however, been made by France. The metro system in Paris is one of the best in the world. France has been making great advance in the technology in its metro system. The latest technological marvel has been achieved beneath the surface of the earth through a concrete cylinder. No one on board is at the controls because there are no controls on board. Instead the sleek good looking aluminum and steel train is being guided by a computer from a distant command centre. Moving at 100 kilometers and hour the them suddenly stops as soon as bright lights appear ahead. Glass door open and the passengers step on an immaculate platform awash in filtered daylight tastefully decorated with mosaics and sculptures.

The train is the remarkable VAL ( Vehicule Automatique Leger), the most ultra –modern futuristic subway system in the world inaugurated in the year 1983 in the Northern French city of Lillie to the nearby cities. This is considered to be the most advanced automatic subway line in the world. VAL is distinguished from most conventional subway systems by its compact size, speed and computerized operating system. Each car is only 6.75 feet wide and 42.6 feet long as compared to 8 feet by 49.2 feet for a Paris metro car. Each train with two cars carries a normal capacity load of 124 passengers in clean, well – lighted comfort.

The system is operated from a remarkable control complex on the outskirts of lille city. Two rows of television form an electronic tableau of the entire system four operators can call up images on the video monitors from 250 cameras installed in stations. Tunnels and garages. The systems computer is programmed to run the trains at a rate of one train every minute during peak hours and every five minutes at other times. the computer is liked to about 200 microprocessors located in the stations and on board the train in case of any misha or accident, VAL operators can stop a train, slow it down or make any of the over 2,000 possible electronic commands.

The trains are equipped with telephones that enable passengers to report any crimes and summon the system's 20-members security force. The driverless system is almost foolproof as is claimed. Indeed, during one of the trial runs, a pigeon alighted on an elevated section of the line, tripping automatic detectors and stopping a train for only ten seconds before its on-board computer ascertained that it was safe to proceed. Railway systems however, may not be abe to indulge in such luxuries for a very long time. However, the importance of computers in railway has been more than emphasized.

## VIDEOTEX SYSTEM

This system was invented by the British Telecom is a way of providing computerized information without the expense of supplying a computer terminal. All that is required is a telephone line and a standard colour television receiver with an adapter to like it to a keyboard and a decoder. The videotext system has been a great help to travel agents and tour operators in their day to day functioning.

Videotext provides efficient, low cost information and reservation facilities which allows direct communications between agents and principle throughout the industry. Information is transmitted quickly and accurately via ordinary telephone line to be visually displayed on a television type screen . at the touch of a button it displays information on holiday packages, airfares accommodations, cruises, car rentals insurance, and many other travel-related services.

The videotext system provides the following services to the travel agent /tour operators.

I.  Fact and efficient means of obtaining accurate, update information on every aspect of the travel industry with excellent visual capacity;
II.  Direct access to the information supplied by industry principals, thereby speeding up transactions and increasing both the efficiency of selling and the quality of customer services
III.  Information on new product developments, fare changes special offers and any other important information put into the system; and
IV.  Display of tour itineraries graphic illustrations of hotels, resort and tourist attraction by selling staff.

Some other videotext system benefits to users include:

a.  Key world – immediate access to a specific piece of information:
b.  Increased sales – more conversation due to immediate access of information;
c.  Increased productivity – more efficient customer servicing;

d. Cost efficient – reduced costs due to greater efficiency of communication
e. Up-to-date information – continued access to an entire library of travel – related information.

Various technological advances discussed have allowed travel agent and tout operators to expand their role and service their clients more efficiently and comprehensively then ever before. The advantages which the use of computers has given to agents are far more than the investments made for installing and using the system. Computers have become an essential part of travel agency operations.

# FOUR

## Transport and Accommodation Introduction

The transport industry has gained a vital place in the global network system and is one of the most important components of the tourism infrastructure. It now becomes easier for people to travel from one place to another because of the various modes of transportation available.The earliest forms of transportation in the ancient times were animals on land and sails on the sea. Travel development from the need to survive, to expand and develop trade to far off countries, and the hunger to capture new lands and territories. This was followed by the use of steams and electricity in the nineteenth century followed by internal combustion engines.Aircraft with the jet engines were introduced in the 1950s. With the development of technology, travel became faster and more and people could travel around the globe.Since tourism involves the movement of people from their places of residence to the places of tourist attractions, every tourist has to travel to reach the places of interest. Transport is, thus, one of the major components of the tourism industry. To develop any place of tourist attraction there have to be proper, efficient, and safe modes of transportation.Transportation is vital to tourism. Studies have shown that tourists spend almost 30 to 40 percent of their total holiday expenditure on transportation and the remaining on food, accommodation, and other activities. This aspect once again highlights the importance of transportation.A tourist can travel by a variety of means. The tourism professional, as well as tourist, should be aware of the various modes of transport available to reach the destination and at the destination.The various mode of transport can be broadly divided into the following three categories:

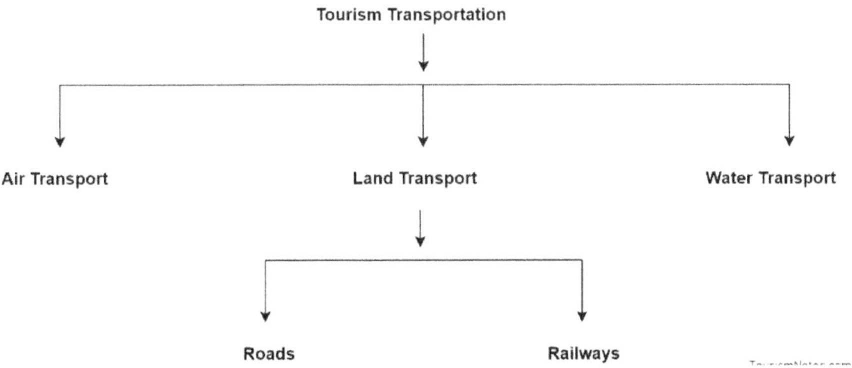


Source Image : https://tourismnotes.com/tourism-transportation/

- Air transport
- Land transport
- Water transport
- Air Transport

Due to the growth of air transport in recent years, long-distance travel has become much simpler and affordable. Distance is now measured in hours and not in kilometers. The world has indeed shrunk and becomes a small village.The development of air transport mostly occurred after World War I and II. Commercial airlines were created for travelers. Because of increasing air traffic, the commercial sector grows rapidly. Before the World War II, Swissair already was carrying around 14-16 passenger between Zurich to London.The first commercial service was introduced by KLM, the Dutch Airlines, in 1920 between Amsterdam and London. Commercial air travel grew mostly after World War II. More facilities were introduced and there was more comfort in travel.Jet flights were inaugurated by Great Britain in the year 1952. In the year 1958 Pan American introduced the Boeing 707 services between Paris and New York. Due to the introduction of jet flights, the year 1959 onward saw a tremendous increase in air traffic. The concept of chartered flights was also introduced during this year.Jumbo jets have revolutionized travel. A large number of people travel by air because of the speed, comfort, and economy in terms of time saved.The modern era, thus, is the era of mass air travel. After road transport, air travel is the most popular mode of travel, particularly for international travel. For the business travelers, air transport is more convenient as it saves their precious time and offers a luxurious and hassle-free travel. Many airlines nowadays offer special facilities to the business tourist such as Internet on board.

There two types of airlines. These are following as:

- Scheduled
- Chartered

Scheduled airlines operate as regular schedules. Chartered airlines or the non-scheduled airlines operate only when there is a demand, mainly during the tourist seasons. The chartered flights work out cheaper than the scheduled carriers as they are operated only when there is a high load factor. Chartered flights provide cheaper packages to the destination such as Portugal and Spain.India receives more than 400 chartered flights, especially to Goa. Goa has a maximum number of chartered flights coming in during the months of December to January.The International Air Transport Association (IATA) regulates international air travel. IATA has more than 105 major airlines of the world as its members. IATA regulates the price of tickets on different sectors of travel in the world. The concerned government decides the domestic fares.The airfares are normally determined on the volume and the air travel demand in an area.The International Civil Aviation Organization (ICAO) is an intergovernmental organization established in the year 1945. Only the government of the country can become a member. The government has to enter into a bilateral agreement for the frequency of flights for operating commercial airlines between them.Airlines are classified into two broad categories namely small carrier and large carrier. The small carrier also known as commuter airlines have less than 30 seats. The larger carriers, also known as major airlines fly direct routes between the major cities and seat and seat 100 to 800 passengers.The recent boom in the aviation technology has certainly bought some new development to airlines industry. There has been a major change in the size of the aircraft.Every year there are a growing number of new airlines being introduced. Because of the growing number of new private airlines, there is stiff competition among them. This has resulted in a considerable reduction in air fairs and has boosted the growth of air traffic. To woo and attract customers, many airlines offer cheaper promotional fares such as excursion fares, group fares, and apex fares.Million of tonnes of cargo and mail are also handled by the air transport industry.

**Road Transport**

Humans travel place to place in search of food in the primitive era. They tamed animals such as the dog, ox, horse, camel, reindeer, elephants, etc. for carrying the load and traveling. After the discovery of the wheel, humans developed the cart, the chariot, and the carriage.Until the seventeenth century, horses were used for traveling. Later on better roads were constructed and some of these roads developed into trade routes, which linked many countries. One of them is the Silk Route which was used for transporting silk from China to Persia and the Blue Gem road from Iran to Afghanistan and India.Today, the most popular and widely used mode of road travel is the automobile or the car. Road transport is dominated by the automobile, which provides views of the landscape and the freedom to travel. Tourist often travels with their entire family for holidays.To promote tourism, the vehicle required are coaches and tourist cars. Tourist coaches or buses are preferred for large tourist groups traveling together on a specified tour itinerary. Many tourists prefer to travel in comfort and privacy and hire cars. Cars of various makes and standards are available on a rental basis.Tourist also uses their own motorcar when holidaying. Cars and coaches carried long distance by train facility is also available in some countries.The car rental segment of the tourism industry is in a very advanced stage in foreign countries. The client can book a car, himself or through agents, and make it wait at the desired place at the destination. The client can then drive the car himself /herself on reaching the destination.

**Rail Transport**

The railway is the most economical, convenient, and popular mode of travel especially for long distance travel all over the world. The railroad was invented in the seventeenth century in Germany with wooden tracks. The first steel rail was developed in the USA during the early 1800s. The railways revolutionized transportation and mass movement of people seen in the nineteenth and twentieth centuries.The broad gauge lines account for more than 55 percent of the total network and carry 85 percent of total traffic. The steam engines have been replaced by diesel and electric engines which have helped in increasing the speed. Railways have promoted tourism by introducing a special tourist train.In Europe, the railway systems of six European countries have been clubbed to make rail travel easier for the people of Europe. A rail passenger can buy a ticket in any one country of Europe and travel through six countries. For the foreign tourists, Eurail Passes offer unlimited discounts travel in express trains for periods ranging from a week to three months. In the USA, AMTRAK operates trains.

**Water Transport**

Humans have been traveling through water since time immemorial and carried good and people from one place to another. The boats progressed from the simple raft with some modifications and improvement and were first used around 6000 BC.Travel by ship was the only means for traveling overseas until the middle of the twentieth century. The Cunard Steamship Company was formed in 1838 with regular steamship services operating on the North Atlantic. During the World War I, in 1914 the operations of the steamship company had to be suspended. After the World War I, the steamship luxury liners were back to business till World War II.After the World War II, the large luxury liners again started their operations all over the world and carried passengers and holidaymakers. Some of the linear were very large accommodating up to 1000 passengers and had facilities like swimming pools, cinema halls, shops, casino, etc.The cruise lines are the new attraction among the tourist. The cruises are booked several months in advance for trips into the tropical and sub-tropical waters of the Hawaii, Caribbean, Mediterranean, etc. Water transport today plays two main roles in travel and tourism namely ferrying and cruising.Modern vessels such as the wave -piercing, the hydrofoil and the hovercraft are the over the water transport and used for short distance routes.Water transportation is also used in riverboat travel. The Mississippi River has been a popular tourist river since the first settlers came to the USA. Today, tourists enjoy two or three-day luxury trips along the river. In Europe, the Rhine, winding through the grapes growing areas of Germany, offers similar leisure tourist trips.Motorized ferries and launches are used over rivers to transport tourists and locals, to transport vehicles, and offer facilities such as car parking, restaurants, viewing decks, etc.Advantages and Disadvantages of Various Modes of TransportTourist has a wide variety of transport options available today.

**4.1 There are several advantages and disadvantages of all the model of transport. These are following as:**

**Air Transport**

Direct root, high speed, quick service, social and political significance, luxurious travel are the advantages of air transportation.

High cost, jet lag, unsuitable for heavy bulk cargo, accidents always fatal, international rule to be observed are the disadvantages of air transportation.

**Road Transport**

Flexibility, reliable, door to door service, economical, supplements other modes of transport, quick transit for short distances are the advantages of road transport.

Slow speed, carrying capacity limited, accidents, none- AC coaches not so comfortable, comfort depends upon the conditions of roads are the disadvantages of road transport.

**Railways**

Long distance travel cheaper, carrying capacity large, dependable service, quicker than road transportation, ability to view scenery en route is the advantage of railways.

Inflexible, unfit to hilly regions, difficulties in rural areas, dining car facilities not always available are the disadvantage of railways.

**Water Transport**

Economical, carrying capacity enormously, develops international and coastal trades are the advantages of water transport.

**4.2 Transportation As An Attraction**

To attract customers as well as take them around an attraction, destination developers have used many forms of transport to move people around. These novel modes of transport ensure that major exhibits are viewed in a certain sequence and ensure that the crowd moves through at a reliable pace.Overcrowding should be avoided at all costs to prevent untoward incidents and to maintain the beauty of the place. Tourist can cover the entire park in a shorter duration with the help of these modes of transport.Transportation is the most crucial component of the tourism infrastructure. It is required not only for reaching the destination but also visiting the site and moving about at the destination. Variety in modes of transportation adds color to the overall tourism experience.Unusual forms of transportation are also an attraction such as the cable cars in hilly terrain, the funicular railway, or jet boating. The choice of mode of transport is vast and tourists can choose a mode to suit their budget. They can opt for scheduled or non-scheduled transport such as the hiring of vehicles, boats, coaches or trains so that they can travel with their group.

## 4.3 CLASSIFICATION OF HOTELS

Grouping hotels based on various criteria is known as classification. Hotel classification serves the following purpose:

- Lends uniformity in services and sets general standards of a hotel
- Provide an idea regarding the range and type of hotels available within a geographical location
- Acts as a measure of control over hotels with respect to the quality of services offered in each category.
- Helps tourist select a hotel that meets their requirement.

CLASSIFICATION ON THE BASIS OF

1. **Size**
2. Location and clientele
3. **Star**
4. Ownership basis
5. **Degree of service offered**

ACCORDING TO SIZE

- SMALL SIZED HOTEL: less then 100 rooms
- MEDIUM SIZED HOTEL: between 100 to 299 rooms
- LARGE SIZED HOTEL: between 300 to 599 rooms
- VER LARGE HOTEL: between 600 to 999 rooms
- MEGA: more than 1000 rooms

ACCORDING TO LOCATION AND CLIENTELE
**DOWNTOWN OR COMMERCIAL HOTEL:**
Location: heart of the city / commercial area or busy business area
Clientele: mostly business man
Facility: modern facilities like 24 hr coffee shop, room service, business centre, travel desk
Avg. duration of stay: 3 to 7 days
TRANSIT HOTEL:
Location: near the port of entry like bus stand, railway station, airport, sea port

Clientele: mostly people who are traveling, layover passengers, tourist, misconnection passengers

Facility: moderate to modern facilities

Avg. duration of stay: few hours too few days

RESORT HOTEL

Location: places with natural beauty like hill station, sea beach, forest

Clientele: mostly holiday makers and tourist Facility: moderate to modern

Avg. duration of stay: a week too few months

MOTEL OR MOTOR HOTEL OR FREEWAY HOTEL:

Location: on highways

Clientele: motorist, tourist travelling by road Facility: moderate to modern facilities

Special features: parking space against each room Refueling station

Garage facility Swimming pool

Avg. duration of stay: mostly over night

SUB- URBAN HOTEL :

Location: outskirts of the city or suburb

Clientele: who have to stay for a longer duration, away from the hustle and bustle of the city

Facility: moderate, budgeted

Avg. duration of stay: longer duration, months

FLOATEL:

Location: lodging properties that float on the surface of water.

4.4 ACCORDING TO STAR CLASSIFICATION/ STANDARD CLASSIFICATION

The Star denotes the standards of the hotel. Department of tourism, govt. of India is responsible for the star gradation. An autonomous body (a committee) is responsible for star gradation of hotels known as Hotel and Restaurant Approval Classification Committee (HRACC), formed by the Ministry of Tourism, Govt. of India. After receiving the application form from hotel HRACC visits the hotel, check the standards and grade the hotel. The Department of Tourism prescribes the facilities which are to be provided in various star category hotels. The term for Star Gradation is for two years.

The six grades of star are

5 Deluxe *

5*

4*

3*

2*

1*

The categories of various star hotels have some criteria or facilities, which are called END.

E – Essentials (have to have)

N – Necessities (should have)

D – Desirables (may or may not have)

Following are the members of HRACC:

- Secretary Tourism, Govt. Of India
- Regional Director of Tourism, Govt. Of India
- One representative from Federation of Hotels and Restaurants Association of India (FHRAI), who is generally the Secretary of the respective zone (of the four zones).
- One representative of the Travel Agents Association of India (TAAI), who is generally the Secretary of the concerned region.
- Director of Tourism of the state concerned
- Principal of the regional Hotel Management Institute.

(If any of the six members is absent on the day of visit, they are permitted to send their own representatives)

HOTEL STAR RATING GUIDE ONE STAR

Typically small hotels , located near affordable attractions, with basic facilities, with a family atmosphere. Limited range and simple facilities and meals. Acceptable standards of maintenance, cleanliness and comfort

TWO STAR

Economy hotel, small to medium size hotel, located near moderately priced attraction. Guest can expect little more than a one star, like comfortable well equipped room with attached bath, professional staff.

THREE STAR

Moderate hotel, spacious accommodation, well equipped room and decorated lobbies, located near business areas, moderate to high price attractions, usually have medium size restaurant that serves breakfast through dinner. Facilities such as direct dial phone, toiletries, Room service, and pool are often provided.

FOUR STAR

first class hotel, large formal hotel, located near major attractions, above average service levels, more than one restaurant, 24 hrs room service, laundry, valet parking, travel desk, wellness center, pool, high class room décor.

FIVE STAR

superior hotel, high level of accommodation and service, large property, hotel lobby and rooms with stylish furnishing and linen, all modern and high end facilities and amenities, at least three restaurant, 24 hrs room service, concierge to assist you 24hrs.

FIVE STAR DELUXE

Highest level of accommodation and service, this hotel provide all 5 star facilities like ultimate decor and high degree of personal service like butler service.

HERITAGE HOTELS

A recent addition to the hotel industry in the country, heritage hotels are properties set in small forts, palaces or havelis. In a heritage hotel, a visitor is offered rooms that have their own history, is served traditional cuisine, is entertained by folk artistes, get a glimpse into the heritage of the region. According to the ministry of tourism, the heritage hotels are further subdivided as follows:

Heritage – built between 1935 and 1950 Heritage classic - built between 1920 and 1935 Heritage grand - built prior to 1920

**5.5 OWNERSHIP BASIS:**

PROPRIETARY OWNERSHIP / INDEPENDENT HOTEL: owners' hotel Proprietary ownership is the direct ownership of one or more properties by a person or company. Small lodging properties are owned by family and large properties are owned by major international hotel companies. No affiliations or contract with other property, No tie up with other hotels. Owner has independent control

Profit goes to the owner. Quickly respond to market changes. Work with limited finances

MANAGEMENT CONTRACTED HOTELS: management by others Properties owned by individuals or partners, operated by external professional organization for management fee.

Adv. – international recognitions, operating systems, training program, marketing, international expertise, profitable operations, advertisement, reservation system, staff.

CHAIN HOTEL: a group of hotels that are owned or managed by one company is called chain hotel.

Adv.: Large central organization providing central reservation system, management aids, financial strength, expertise, manpower, specialties, promotions

FRANCHISE HOTELS/ AFFILIATED:

It is the authorization given by a company to another company or individual to sell its unique products and services and use its trademark according to the guidelines given by the former , for a specified time and at a specified place.

Franchise owner (franchisor) grant another hotel( franchisee) the right use its methods & system, technical services, marketing trademark, signs etc. for fees.

Adv.-Opening assistance- architectural, interior designs Systems and procedure

Staff training Financial assistance

Advertising and global marketing Central reservation

Central purchase

REFERRAL CHAIN:

A referral chain is made up of independently owned and operated hotel and provides shared advertisement, joint reservation system and standardized quality. Virtually there is no shared management or financial functions

TIME SHARE / VACATION OWNERSHIP/ HOLIDAY OWNERSHIP: Each room is owned by several people for different time period. Each owner gets a stay of specific period for a number of years.

One time purchase is made by paying purchase price & payment of a yearly maintenance fee.

Generally located at dream sites like beaches, hill, waterfall etc.

Adv.- long term accommodation, comfort homes, economical, good location, international exchange possible.


· CONDOMINIUM:

Joint ownership of a complex.

Type of accommodation where owner of a room or an apartment in a complex, of several such accommodations, furnishes it and informs the management of the times when he will be using it. He permits to rent out the apartments at other times and the rent goes to the owner. The owner pays the monthly maintenance fee.

5.6 DEGREE OF SERVICE OFFERED

UPMARKET/ LUXURY/ WORLD CLASS SERVICEHOTELS

Targeting the affluent segment of society, hotels in the up market category offer world class products with personalized service of the highest standards. The emphasis is on excellence and class. These hotel provides upscale restaurant and lounges, exquisite décor, concierge service, abundant amenities.

MID MARKET/ MIDSEGMENT SERVICE HOTELS

These hotels offer modest services without the frill and personalized attention of luxury hotels, and appeal to the largest segment of travelers. they offer services such as room service, round the clock coffee shop, pick up drop, multi cuisine restaurant and bar.

BUDGET OR ECONOMY HOTELS OR LIMITED SERVICE

Focus on meeting the most basic needs if guests by providing clean, comfortable and inexpensive rooms. Hotels have clean and comfortable guest rooms , coffee shop, a multi cuisine restaurant , in room telephone and channeled music and movies, swimming pool, health club.

CLASSIFICATION ON THE BASIS OF CLIENTELE:

- BUSINESS OR COMMERCIAL HOTEL: cater to the business traveller, generally situated in the city Centre.
- TRANSIENT HOTEL: cater to the needs of people who are on the move and need a stopover en route their journey, situated in close proximity of ports of entry.

- RESIDENTIAL HOTEL: cater to the guest who stays for a long duration.

- CASINO HOTEL: casino hotel provide gambling facilities.

- CONFERENCE HOTEL: hotel cater and organize conference

- CONVENTION HOTEL: who organize convention and cater to the guest who come to attend the convention.

- SANATORIA: hotel which has health club and spa, and caters to the people who came to these spas for treatment.

## CLASSIFICATION ON THE BASIS OF DURATION OF GUEST STAY:

- COMMERCIAL HOTEL: duration of stay is short, usually 1-7 days
- TRANSIENT HOTEL: duration of stay from few hours to 1 day
- SEMI RESIDENTIAL HOTEL: duration of stay range from few weeks to some months
- RESIDENTIAL / APARTMENT HOTEL: duration of stay range from months to few years
- EXTENDED STAY HOTEL: duration of stay few days to weeks.

OTHERS

**CITY CENTER HOTEL:**

By virtue of their location, meet the needs of the traveling public for business or leisure reasons. These hotels could be luxury, business, economy or residential.

AIRPORT HOTEL:

Hotel located near the airport, clientele mainly consist of travelers arriving and departing from airport. Facilities include 24 hrs coffee shop and room service.

CASINO HOTEL:

Serves guest who want to gamble and have a casino. Not very popular in India. In addition to gaming, a multi cuisine restaurants, spa, dance club etc are also available.

CONVENTION HOTEL:

Hotel provides facilities and meets the needs of group attending and holding conventions and conferences. Have much banquet area, meeting rooms in and around hotel complex. Facilities include 24 hrs room service, in house laundry, travel desk, airport shuttles twin bedded rooms.

APARTOTEL:

Apartment building also used as a residential hotel. Purchase of hotel entitles full service of hotel, when not occupied , it is added in the hotel pool to earn revenue.

BOUTIQUE:

Small, expensive, informal atmosphere, gives personal service, all outlet has different theme. All rooms have different theme and decoration.

AUBERGE, GASTHOF, HERBERGE:

Small units like inn which provide complimentary bar, restaurant and bedroom for travelers. Emphasis is given on eating and drinking facilities.

BORDING HOUSE/ PENSION:

Accommodation usually with meals for a definite period of time commonly for a week or more. Also know as guest house, or pension.

HOLIDAY VILLAGE:

Hotel that provide accommodation with other facilities like recreation, sports facilities, individual kitchen, green zone, library, nursery, television room, landscaping.

PALACE HOTEL:

Indian concept, maharajas palaces are converted into hotels, gives old heritage, architecture, modern facilities in traditional style, and traditional way of service.

MATELS:

Fully automated hotels which require minimum human contact. Online booking, self check in, check out, outsourced cleaning crew.

SANATORIA:

Found at spas and health resorts. Rooms equipped with sauna, Jacuzzi. Meals are personalized diet regimes of the guest. Hotel has dietician, doctors and medical arrangements.

## 6.7 OTHER TYPES OF ACCOMMODATION / SUPPLEMENTARY ACCOMMODATION

Supplementary Accommodation can be described as premises which offer accommodation but not the extra services of a hotel. It plays a very important role in the total available tourist accommodation in the country. It caters to both international and domestic tourist traffic. Main distinguishing features are:

1. The standard of comfort is moderate to that of a hotel.
2. They sell accommodation at much lower price.
3. They have an informal atmosphere.

CAMPS:

Usually located on the trekking routes. Prove parking space, common toilets, tents, camp fire, and other basic services.

YOUTH HOSTEL:

Have dormitory style accommodation, common toilets, dinning areas, simple food, fixed menu, and gym and sports area

PAYING GUEST:

Guest pays and stays with the owner for a longer duration, food and accommodation provided.

GOVERNMENT HOUSES:

Also known as Dak Bungalows, Circuit houses, Forest lodges and PWD houses. Set in British raj for different reasons. Have a local person as caretaker who cooks, cleans, assist and provide security. Initially Dak bungalows were used for postal and courier service, circuit house for higher ranked officers, forest house for forestry officials and PWD house for road and electricity department officials.

FLOATEL:

Hotels built on the water surface, do not move, docked at ports. Provide exclusive and exotic atmosphere.

BOATELS:

Floating hotels, takes passengers from one place to another. Provide food and accommodation.

ROTELS:

Accommodation on wheels is known as Rotels. Different types of Rotels are caravans, palace on wheels and new sleeper buses.

HOSPICES:

Traditional lodges in Europe for Christian pilgrims to Jerusalem. Provide meditation centers & prayer rooms, food etc. in India we find DHARMSHALA.

GUEST HOUSE:

Small place which provide basic boarding and lodging services.

DORMITORIES:

A room with several beds, toilets is in end of the corridor.

HOLIDAY HOMES:

Small accommodation, affiliated to companies meant for the company people to go and stay.

**Time share Hotels**

Time share properties involve individuals who purchase the ownership of accommodations for a specific period of time- usually one or two weeks a year. These hotels are very popular in resort areas.

Condominium Hotels

The difference between the time - share and condominium hotels lies in the type of ownership. Units in condominium hotels (A condominium is a unit consisting of a living room, dining area, kitchen, bathroom and one or more bedrooms) only have one owner instead of multiple owners. In a condominium hotel, an owner informs the management company of when he or she wants to occupy the unit. The management company is free to rent out the unit of the remainder of the year. Condominium owners receive revenue from the rental of their units and pay the management company a fee for advertising, rental, housekeeping and maintenance services.

# FIVE

# Marketing and Tourism Concepts

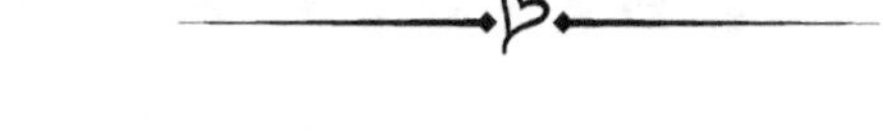

Marketing is one of the most important functions of management. Marketing teaches you the techniques and strategies to promote products and services. Marketing management is concerned with the skills to analyse, plan, coordinate and implement various strategies towards the accomplishment a customer's requirements and the firm's objectives. In a highly competitive market like tourism, you would be interested to improve your market share and expand your business. You must remember that in tourism you are required not only to sell tourism services but also dreams. You must be fully equipped to do the job keeping in view the objectives of your organisation and its customers. This, you can do better through a proper understanding of marketing management. This is precisely what will be discussed in this lesson. It will introduce you to the concept of marketing, its application in tourism, the nuances of marketing functions, marketing environment, pricing strategies, advertising, channels of distribution, management of customer relationship.

After studying this lesson, you will be able to:

- discuss the concept and Functions of Marketing for Tourism
- describe the role of Marketing Environment for Tourism
- discuss Pricing Strategies
- recognise Advertising and Sales Promotion
- identify Distribution Channels for Marketing and
- describe the role of Customer Relationship Management.

# 5 CONCEPT AND FUNCTIONS OF MARKETING

https://quizizz.com/admin/quiz/5ff7e7e7b2fe60001ca21723/marketing-functions

Human activities can be broadly divided into two categories— economic and non-economic activities. Economic activities are performed to earn livelihood such as business, employment or a profession. Business, being an economic activity, is carried out primarily with an aim to earn profits. A business organisation is involved in providing goods and services to consumers. Any business would be useless if the goods produced are not sold in the market. The success of a business organisation largely depends on how efficiently the products and services are delivered to the customers. In order to make the products available to consumers, number of activities such as product designing, packaging, warehousing, transportation, branding, advertising, pricing and selling are required. So the sum total of all those activities that direct the flow of goods and services from producers to consumers is referred to as marketing.

**Tourism Marketing**

The success of any segment of travel and tourism industry depends on how well the products and services are marketed. Tourism being a service industry, marketing of services is different from most of the products because what is being sold is an experience rather than a tangible product. Tourism marketing is concerned about understanding the needs of its potential customers (tourists) and satisfying those needs by offering a suitable product. In this section we will briefly discuss some features of tourism products.

1. **Inseparability**: Services are consumed and experienced by a customer simultaneously and as such makes it impossible to demonstrate the product being offered before it is actually consumed. For example, a tourist who is travelling from Delhi to Mumbai will consume the services offered by the airline and at the same time feel the experience.

2. **Perishability**: This is another important aspect of tourism products. Tourism products are intangible in nature and cannot be stored like the other tangible products. For example, if a bus having a capacity of 50 seats leaves with 30 filled seats only, the vacant seats cannot be stored and therefore become useless or so to say they perish.

3. **Ownership:** In tourism products, a customer buys only the experience. The transfer of ownership does not take place. For example in case of tourism products like hotels, houseboats and aeroplanes, the customer experiences only the stay in a hotel or a house boat but does not own the product.

4. **Heterogeneity:** The other aspect of tourism products is their heterogeneity. Tourism products are a combination of several services provided by people. The high involvement of humans' results in variation in behaviour from one consumer to another. For example, an employee at a bank counter, may not behave in the same manner with every customer.

**Functions of Marketing**

An organisation before achieving its desired goals has to go through a series of marketing functions. The understanding of marketing functions or marketing tasks becomes very essential to understand the subject of marketing. In this section we will discuss marketing functions which can be considered as a system where interaction occurs between an organisation and a customer.

The main marketing functions or tasks of marketing are discussed with special reference to tourism marketing. The functions are as follows:

a. Market Research.

b.  Product Planning and Development.
c.  Segmentation.
d.  Promotion.
e.  Selling.

## 5.1 NEED FOR MARKETING IN TOURISM

Tourism is the fastest growing industry in the world and therefore the need for marketing it becomes imperative. Tourism needs to be marketed just as any other product, indeed more so, because it is an industry where the customer still has an immense variety of choice. The choice for the holiday market is wide as more and more countries and resorts throughout the world expend their tourism industries.

**DEFINING TOURISM MARKETING**

Tourism marketing can be defined as the "systematic and coordinated efforts exerted by the national tourist organizations and / or the tourism enterprises at international, national and local levels to optimize the satisfaction of tourists, group and individuals, in view of the sustained tourism growth." according to Krippendrof. J., marketing in tourism means " Systematic and coordinated excursion of business policy by tourist undertakings whether private or state owned at local, regional, national or international level to achieve the optimal satisfaction of the needs of identifiable consumer groups, and in doing so to active and appropriate return.

**THE TOURST PRODUCT**

Availability of a 'product' is the prerequisite in the marketing function. Unless there is a certain 'product', be it tangible or intangible or a service, marketing is not possible. A product may be defined as the sum of the physical and psychological satisfactions it provides to the buyer. Marketing by definition is the development of a product to meet the needs of the consumer and then employing the techniques for direct sales, publicity and advertising to bring this product to the consumer.

For a tourist product, the basic raw materials are the country's natural beauty climate, history, culture and the people. Other aspect are the existing facilities necessary for comfortable living such as water supply, electricity, roads, transport, communication and other essentials in other words the tourist product can be seen as a composite product as the sum total of a countries tourist attraction transport accommodation and the entertainment which hopefully result in consumer satisfaction. The tourist product can be entirely a man-made one or nature's creation improved upon by man. Each of these components of a tourist product is supplied by individual provides of service like hotel companies, airlines or other suppliers, and is offered directly to the tourist by them. A consumer can combine these individual tourist products through a large number of ways. There would be many possible destination each with a number of hotels each to be reached by more than one airline thus the potential choose before the consumer is very large

The tourist product can therefore, be analyzed in terms of:-

a. Attractions
b. Facilities
c. Accessibilities

Of the three basic components of a tourist product 'attractions' are very important. Useless these are there; the tourist will not be motivated to go to a particular place. Attractions are those elements in the tourist to visit on particular destination rather than another.

### 5.2 SPECIAL FEATURES OF TOURISM MARKETING

Although general principles of marketing of products of other industries could be applicable to marketing of tourist product, there are certain differences are because of the peculiar character of the tourist product. The following are the peculiarities of a tourist product.

Intangible non-material

No transfer of ownership of goods is involved as compared to a tangible product.

Production and consumption closely interrelated

The travel agent or tour operator who sells his product cannot store it production can only be completed if the customer is actually present.

Assembled by many producers

The tourist product cannot be provided by a single enterprise. Each of the components of a tourist product is highly specialized and together makes the final product

Highly unstable demand

The demand is influenced by factors such as seasonal demands, economy, political reasons, etc., the seasonal change greatly affect the demand. Seasonality means the tourism plant is frequently used for a limited part of the year and therefore uneconomic.

Dominant role of intermediaries

In tourism, sales intermediaries like tour operators, travel agents, reservation service and hotel brokers lay a very dominant role and enjoy superior and hotel brokers play a very dominant role and enjoy superior marketing strength. From the standpoint of tourism marketing, this strong position of the travel trade has significant implications.

**Divers motivations**

Choice for a certain holiday destination, type of accommodation and vacation activities are far less evident. Very often two people make exactly the same choices for entirely different and sometimes even mutually exclusive reasons.

**Marketing process**

Initially, supply being short of demand it used to be mainly the sales management function as distinct from the market management function. The rapid industrial advancement subsequently placed at the disposal of the consumer a large variety of goods of improved quality and in abundant quantity from a large number of competing manufacturers resulting in supply exceeding demand. This compelled the manufacturers to give greater consideration to the marketing concept.

The marketing concept in the field of tourism comprises the following major processes or functions:

   I.  Market research
  II.  Product formulation and development
 III.  Product distribution
 IV.  Advertising
  V.  Sales promotion or support and
 VI.  Public relations

## 5.3 MARKETING RESEARCH

For successful marketing, market research is paramount. It relates to providing answers to various questions pertaining to the marketing activities. Market research can be defined as the 'systematic collection of information relating to supply and demand for a product or a proposed product in such a way that the information may be used by the organized to formulate informed decisions about its policies and its objectives.

Research techniques:

There are various methods used to collect the data. Among the variety of methods used, some seed to be widely resorted to because of their advantages over others. Research techniques can be grouped as:

1.  Desk research
2.  Field research
3.  Motivation research

## *Desk research*

Desk research includes the collection and analysis of all available data Statistics and published information on tourist trends and markets. In tourism much of the basic information about tourist trends and markets is available from existing sources. There are a number of international organizations like united nations, UNESCO,UIOTO,WTO,IEC,IATA,PATA,ICAO., etc., which publish statistical information. Other data and statistics may be obtained from national tourist organizations, carriers, hotel companies, etc., this information proves very useful in assisting national tourist organizations to identify their markets and determine the objectives. The published information is of particular use to those countries which do not possess resources enough to undertake independent market research.

**Field research:-**

Field research on the other hand is the research work carried out in the tourist generating markets itself. The special investigations in the field are to be carried out with a view to know more details of the market situation. Field research includes methods among which the most common are sample surveys and the motivation research.

**Surveys:-**

Sample survey could be defined as the study of a given population through only a part or a fraction thereof much marketing information is obtained through the use of samples.

**Motivation Research:-**

Motivation research attempts to describe and the motives of the population under investigation, by use of techniques originally used in psychology. Assuming that every individual knows what he wants, motivation research is oriented to discover the needs of potential tourists in over to adopt the tourist supply accordingly and thus be able to satisfy them.

**Marketing Strategy:-**

Developing a sound tourist marketing is the next logical step after having identified the markets. It may, however, be mentioned here that the market research, as a continuous process of investigating market conditions is just a means to an end which is to develop a marketing strategy.

Market may be described "as a place where buyers and sellers of goods and services meet and between them the exchange transaction takes place". It may be used in connection with a particular geographical area or in connection with a particular type of service or product. The 'market' therefore can be defined as "the totally of actual and or potential buyers of a given product of service in a specified geographical location at a given point in time of during a given period of time".

Market segmentation is the process of identifying groups of buyers of a total market with different buying desires or requirements.

The main objectives of market segmentation are:

I. Developed new markets for product variations of new products;
II. Developing defense against competitors by differentiating one's own product from their and matching it more closely to requirements of a particular segments of market;
III. Achieving maximum effects for given expenditure on marketing activities particularly communication activities;
IV. Developing marketing programme and budget on the basic of a clearer idea of the response characteristics of specific segments

The information on the tourists markets which will assist in segments are:

1. Income distributions of over seas travelers and particularly correlation between income and distance traveled and travel expenditure on travel;
2. Travel expenditure data i.e. distribution of per head expenditure on travel;
3. Discretionary income of households, correlated with other characteristics enabling target to be identified closely;
4. Historical trends in the different socio-economic categories;
5. Survey data on attitudes to and motivation for overseas travel;

6.  Geographical dispensation of potential customers within the market;
7.  Membership of the clubs and association associated with other characteristics which identify particular groups as potential customer
8.  Influenced of intermediaries (travel agent, tour operator, wholesalers, carriers, etc) on destinations choice in particular markets; and
9.  Relative importance of different intermediaries in particular market.

## 5.4 MARKET TARGETING

One of the early in marketing tourism is to divide the present and potential market on the basis of meaningful characteristics and then concentrate on promotion, supply and market pricing efforts on serving these most prominent sections of the market the target market.

A.  The Vocation Tourist

The vacation or the holiday tourist is the most common and popular tourists. He is immensely affected by the changes in price, and is easily influenced by the skilled and aggressive marketing efforts this of tourist is resort-oriented the vacation tourist market has been regarded as highly seasonal.

A.  The Business Tourist

In recent years the market for this type of tourist has increased greatly. The choice of destination of a business tourist is generally determined by the business. The marketing efforts will not influence much the choice of the business tourist. As in case of vacation tourist who has proved to be very sensitive to price changes the demand for business tourism is relatively price-inelastic. The demand will tend to be big city oriented. The visits are of shorter duration and relatively frequent. The trade fairs, conventions, exhibitions, conferences and similar other events attract this kind of tourists

C.  The Common Interest Tourist

This segment comprises visits to relatives and friends and visits for the purpose of education, for pilgrimage etc. the demand for this type of tourism will be relatively price-elastic. The common interest tourist will not be easily influenced by the promotional efforts. The average length of stay of this type of tourist will be relatively longer. Because of his friends and relatives, he will not be a significant user of hotel and other types of accommodation. The visits will not be frequent and expenditure relatively little on his stay as compared with two groups.

## TOURISM PROMOTION

In order to market a product, it is necessary that information about the product reaches a prospective consumer. As applied to tourism industry, the most important function of marketing is to bring about an awareness of the product in the minds of existing as well as prospective consumer in the overall market area. All this forms a part of overall tourism promotion. The basic function of all tourism promotional activities is to have an effective and meaningful communication with the consumer and trade intermediaries. This is possible through certain identifiable methods which are being practiced by all the marketing organizations. The awareness is brought about through certain methods/marketing tools these are:

a.  Advertising
b.  Public Relations

The above tools are, however, not exclusive but complementary to each other. Proper and judicious blend of these is essential for the successful marketing of a tourism product.

## ADVERTISING

Advertising is a non-personal communication of a sales message to actual or potential purchasers of a product by a person or an organization selling a product or a service. The sales message is delivered through a paid medium for the purpose of influencing the buying behaviour of those purchasers. The term may be defined "any activity designed to spread information with a view to promoting the sales of marketable goods and services". As such it operates in two ways; firstly spreading information among consumers, about the possibilities of consumption, and secondly, by seeking to influence their judgment in favour of the particular goods which are the subject of the advertisement. Use of certain paid media space is, however, a prerequisite. A message in the paid media must have as its purpose sale of a product or a service.

Advertising is an investment and like all investment. It should product measurable results. The first and foremost reason for setting advertising objectives is therefore, to measure the return on one's advertising objectives investment. The second reason is that with the availability of many alternative methods for marketing, production and with the availability of many alternative methods for marketing production and with customers becoming more and more value – conscious, organizations must seek the most efficient way of marketing the goods and services if they are to remain competitive.

Professor Robert Buzzell of the Harvard business school, gives the following example of possible advertising objectives for a consumer product advertising to increase sales directly by:

I. Encouraging potential purchasers to visit dealers or distributors.
II. Announcing special sales, contests or other promotions
III. Securing new dealers or distributors
IV. Inducing professional persons (eg: doctors, architects) to recommend a product and
V. Distributing coupons to be redeemed on purchases

To create awareness and interest in the company's product by:

I. Informing potential buyers about product features
II. Announcing the availability of new products
III. Demonstrating the benefits of a product's use
IV. Comparing a product with competing product
V. Showing how a product should be used
VI. Informing potential buyers about the company's technical skills, production facilities,technical services etc.,
VII. Informing purchasers about where products can be obtained
VIII. Announcing changes in prices, packages,labels etc., and
IX. Publicizing a new brand name or symbol

## MEDIA SELECTION

The selection of the medium or media will depend upon the factors like the area to be covered, the type of audience to be reached,the appeals to be made and upon the services and facilities of the particular medium in relation to costs. The important factors which influence the media selection are:

a. Coupon response: answer – back coupons, with some inducement, are incorporated in many advertisement. The amount of response is an indication of the effectiveness of the concerned advertisement.

b. Recall: here the respondents are shown the magazine cover or any other media vehicle in which the concerned advertisement had appeared. They are then asked to tell which advertisements in that publication they remember.

c. Recognition test: here the respondents are shown the advertisement and sked if they have read them.

d. Sales tests: here, the actual sales results before and after the concerned advertising are examined. The sales results in the selected 'test markets' are also compared to those in some chosen 'control marketing', i.e the markets where the concerned advertising is not done. In the field of tourism, advertising is mainly used to create awareness and interest in the tourist service of destination to be promoted and motivates potential tourists to decide to make further enquiries about costs, bookings, facilities etc.,

## 5.5 PUBLICRELATION TECHNIQUES

Public relations make use of several communication techniques. These includes:

1. news and feature stories
2. press releases
3. films and slides
4. booklets and brochures
5. photographs, displays and exhibits
6. advertising
7. house journals
8. news letters
9. stockholder reports

public relations consist of a number of interrelated activities oriented towards creating and maintaining a favourable positive image for the tourist product. The main tools of public relations in tourist promotion are as following:

1. organising familiarisation tours for travel writer, editors, travel agents, photographers and the other key personnel from different parts of the world as guests to visit the country and to get first – hand knowledge about it. These persons then write about the country visited in the well-known travel and other general interest magazines.
2. organizing radio and television contests featuring the destination country.
3. organizing press releases and arranging press conferences with key personnel connected with the tourist field with a view to disseminate information about the destination.
4. arranging seminars and workshops at a place where the tourist promotion office is located.
5. organizing cultural programmes, musical and folk shows, TV interviews exhibitions and national friendship weeks in the country where the national tourist offices is located.
6. organizing various types of contest about the country.
7. encouraging large departmental stores, organizers of fashion shows and manufacturing companies to project the country or a part of the country as a promotion showcase in their premises.

The development of an organized travel as we known it today had its roots in the mid nineteenth century and can be associated with a man know as Thomas cook. Any discussion on sales and organization of travel must make reference to this pioneer. The history of the business of the present. Thomas cook group limited cab be traced back to over 155 years to its founder Thomas cook, who not only can be said to have invented the travel and tourism business as we know it today.

A Baptist preacher and a book salesman of Derbyshire were on his way to a temperance meeting in Leicester to Southborough in England and back to attend a quarterly delegate meeting. He though that it was a sounder proposition to persuade a railway company, then in its infancy, to carry a train- load of passengers at a very cheap fare than to run the train at 'standard' fares, but possibly only a quarter full. His idea was put into operation with characteristic sped and efficiency; as few weeks later 570 travelers made the journey by the midland counties railway at a specially reduced fare. This venture was soon followed by taken on a trip from Leicester to derby in England, perhaps the largest organized group of the time.

Thomas cook's beginning as 'mass excursionist' was, however, the Liverpoor-caernaryon trip 1845. The tourists traveled by rail to live pool, from where they took a steamer to caernaryon. The advertisement for the trip caused a sensation and the response was so overwhelming that a second trip had to be arranged. Cook thought of every detail. He made a preliminary survey of accommodation and facilities and produces a handbook of the trip to Liverpool. The excursionist invasion of Scotland soon followed in 1846 and 1848 to 1863 cook conducted circular tours of Scotland with 5,000 tourists a season, and with sitadels if the landed aristocracy falling before him, cook saw more enticing prospects opening before him. "I had become so thoroughly imbued with the tourist spirit that I began to contemplate foreign trips, including the continent of Europe, the united states and the eastern lands of the bible".

**Grand circular tour:**

By the mid-nineteenth century 'Holiday away from Home' had become customary for a larger social group that ever before. Cook's initiative and organizing genius provided the final impetus. In the winter of 1850-51, cook was already negotiating for a tour of America, but his attention was diverted when he was offered the opportunity of conducting excursion trains to the Great Exhibition of 1851, altogether, Cook conducted 1,65,000 people to an from the Crystal Palace. In 1856, Cook succeeded in organizing his first grand circular tour of the continent. The tour was so successful that it had to be repeated six weeks later.

**Cook's conquest of Europe**

Thomas cook's conquest of Europe began in 1862 when he made arrangements with Brighton and South Coast Railway for passenger traffic to the continent. It was the beginning of his conquest of Europe as a holiday destination and package tours. Cook's Paris excursions are the first True 'package tours'; all the details of transport and accommodation were pre-arranged. In 1863 cook visited Switzerland where his ideas were greeted with enthusiasm by hoteliers and railway proprietors. His next stop was Italy. Cook first made a personal survey of turin, Mailan, Florence and Genoa, to familiarize himself with their tourist attractions and facilities. In 1864 the first guided tour to Italy left England with application far in excess of the available ticket. The 1860s also saw the introduction of cook's railway and hotel coupons cook personally examined the system by traveling through Italy to Vienna, down the Danube into Hungary and form there into Switzerland. By the 1890s 1,200 hotels throughout the world accepted his coupons. Starring in 1868 cook arranged regular circular tours to Switzerland and Northern Italy.

**Cook's oversea Efforts :**

Thomas cook and sons established their first official London office in the year 1865. John mason cook now joined his father as a permanent partner and took in charge of the London office. From that year on the history of Thomas cooks and sons was one of continuous expansion. In the year 1880 john mason cook left for India and established office in Bombay and Calcutta and formed the 'eastern Princes' Department in 1887 which arranged the visits of Indian princes of queen victor's jubilee celebrations.

Taking advantage of nineteenth century advances in transport technology, Thomas cook and sons had effected a revolution in tourism by the end of century. No longer the reserve of the rich and the aristocrats, tourism was now an industry. Armed with cook's hotel and rail coupons, the tourist could demand uniform prices and standardization had distinct advantages. It meant comfort and convenience and less need for decision making on the part of the individual tourist. The tourist was less likely to9 experience or embarrassment. In the year 1898 the management of the company was passed on to john mason cook's three son. At the time of john mason cook's death, the cook's business included three main aspects of travel-selling tours, banking and shipping. Soon after the second world war, the British government acquired the principal interest in the company. In the year 12972, the British government sold the company to midland bank consortium.

Today, Thomas cook group is the parent company of a worldwide group of companies which are partially or wholly owned. The company also has a close trading relationship with Comanie international des wagons-list et du tourism, and the combined worldwide network of these companies, together with their authorized agent. The company also introduced traveler's cheques which were originally called circular notes. Members of the Thomas cook group of companies now issu chjeques as principals in five currencies, and are associated with partner banks in many more currencies. It is also a large trader in the buying and selling of foreign currency bank notes.

Today, the Thomas cook group limited provides a wide range of services to its customers in over 150 countries worldwide through their network of over 1,200 outlets. The company is considered to be one of the largest travel companies selling a wide range of travel services.

## AMERICAN EXPRESS

The American express company also had its beginning in the year 1841. it is an interesting coincidence, that the world's two largest travel companies is said to have their origins in the same year-1841. while Thomas cook persuaded a railway company to carry a train load of passengers at very cheap fares in the year, Henry Wells started his freight business initially as a shopper who later formed the well know company of America known as well Fargo. The American express company, popularly know today as AMEXO, is the world's second largest travel agency after Thomas cook. Besides selling package tours, the company deals in travelers cheques. The American express company is major participant in internations transactions buying and selling huge amounts in foreign currency on each working day of a week.

The company has also introduce American express credit cards. these credit cards are very popular internationally. The services one can buy through these cards are varied and includes purchase of international air tickets, payment of hotel bills among many others. The cards have wide acceptance throughout the world. The company also handles services for various types of insurance, including travels insurance.

## COX KINGS

Cox & kings is another company associated with travel business. Although the company had its origin in the year 1758 earlier than when Thomas cook on the scene, the company's activities initially were associated with the handling of the affairs of British officers stationed overseas.

The history of Cox & Kings stretches back to the appointment by colonel lord Ligonier in 1758 of Richard Cox as regimental agent to the food guard. Cox & co's efficient handing of the affairs of the officers stationed as agent and banker had been extended to the household brigade, many of the cavalry and infantry regiments, the royal artillery and royal wagon train. The company's responsibilities increased steadily, including serving prestigious ships of the Royal Navy, the Royal Flying corps and by the year 1918 the newly formed Royal Air Force.

With the rapid development of the British Empire, Cox & Co. Expanded from its base in London to establish overseas offices. To service the garrisons spread throughout India. Cox & Co. entered into banking and later shipping and forwarding . some of the more interesting assignments included the shipping of the Indian sections of the great London exhibitions of 1851 and 1924, the movement of Wellington's officers and logistics involved in the

Chinese and African exhibitors.

By the year 1918 Co& Co had become an international corporation employing more than 4,500 people in 1922 the company merged with Henry S.Kings a banking concern. In the 1923 the banking business was sold Lloyds bank and the Cox & Kings branch , as the company is known today, was opened the fully integrated Anglo-Indian company Cox & king today has the comprehensive network of local agents offering a wide range of travel services to their client.

## 5.7 TRAVEL AGENCY OPERATION

Much has changed this year 1840, when Thomas cook chartered train to carry 570 travellers at a specially reduced fare from Leicester to lough borough in England. Cook, who brought the railway tickets in bulk and resold them to member of his group can be credited with being the first bona fide travel agent toa work as a full time proposal. However, neither Thomason cook & sons, nor American express company or Cox & king were then a retail agent as the modern complex distribution chain had not yet evolved in any trade including travel.

### SCOPE AND ROLE OF RETAILERS

The scope of the role of these three companies was also limited in the beginning since mass tourism as we know it today had not yet began. It was however, the introduction of the air travel which gave a boost to the travel agency business. The introduction of the economy class by various airlines companies crossing the north atlantic heralded the era of travel agency and was responsible for growth the introduction of an economy class in effect was nothing more thatn a projection of Thomas cooks original idea of the adjusted prices to the encourage full capacity use of every means of transport.

Continuing the development of the transport system, especially the travel improved liding standards combined with reduction in working hours which is the root cause of todays upward surge in travels side by side with the rapid improvements in industries and technology, practically all aspects of life had become more and more.

The travel industry developed along certain well defined lines as the world wide demand on its service increased the large to travel became very intense over the year resulting in wide-spread growth of travel agency in the world most of the travelers wished to have their travel arrangements made in advance and to be relived of the difficulties of coping with various pre travel arrangement of which they had only very limited knowledge.

## MODERN TRAVEL AGENCIES

Over the year the range and activities of retail travel agent have increased manifold. In the modern context the role of a travel agent is rather different to that of most of other retails selling merchandiser the travel agent does not purchase travel with a view to reselling the same to its customers. It is only when a customer has finally decided on the purchase of travel that the agent approaches the principal on behalf of his customer. The retail travel agent unlike most other retailers does not carry an inventory or stock of travel products in his premises.

The main role of retail travel agents is to provide to their customers a convenient location ofr the purchase of various elements of travel like transport accommodation and several other ancillary services associated with holiday and travel. The travel agents acts as booking agents for holiday and travel and disseminate information and give advise on such services this role can be summed up as follows.

a. To give advice to the potential tourist on the merits of alternative destination and
b. To make necessary arrangements for a chosen holiday which may involve booking of accommodation, transport or other relevant services associated with his travel.

A travel agent, is order to his potential customers on the merits of the destination must poseess knowledge expertise and an up to date information about the destination nesides a travel agent has close contacts with provider of service, i.e, their principal from whom they purchase services for their customer in other wards, a retail travel agent is an intermediary providing a direct link between the customer and the supplier of the tourists services, i.e. airlines transport companies, hotels, auto rental companies, etc. The retail agent is the one who acts on behalf of the principal, i.e., the original provider of tourist service such as an airline company, hotel company, shipping company, insurance company, railways or a tour operator. An agent sells the principal's services and is rewarded by a commission.

## 5.8 TRAVEL AGENCY OPERATIONS

The scope and range of travel agency operations would depend on the size of an agency if the company is large in size, the range of activities will be more comprehensive. In this case the agency will have specialized departments, cash having to perform different functions to deal with the subject of a travels agency, the best method of approach is, perhaps to consider the function of a travel agency. These may be broad classified as follows

a. Provision of travel information

One of the primary functions of a retail agent from the point of view of the tourist or the general public is to provide necessary information about trave. This information is provided at a convenient location where the intending tourist may ask certain questions and seek clarifications about his proposed travel. This is very specialized job and the person behind the counter should be a specialist having excellent knowledge of various travel alternate plans. He should be in a position to give up-to date and accurate information regarding various services and general information about travel, etc., The presentation to the potential customer must be forceful, and exciting variations must continually be devised to help sell tours. A good travel agent is something of a personal counselor who knows all the details about the travel and also the nneeds and interests of the intending traveler. Communication plays a key role in dissemination of any type of information. The person behind the travel counter should be able to communicate with the customer in his language. The knowledge of foreign languages is an essential prerequisite for personnel working in a travel agency.

a. Preparation of itineraries

Tourist itinerary is a composition of a series of operations that are a result of the study of the market. A trourist is and , above all, the intricacies of exchange control regulations, which vary from country to country.

Provision of Foregin Currencies:

Proviosion of foreign currencies ot intending travelers is another specialized activity of a travel agency. Some of the larger travel agencies deal exclusively in the provision of foreign currencies, travelers as it saves them a lot of time and energy avoiding visits to regular banking channels.

**INSURANCE**

Inssurance both for personal accident risks and of baggage, is yet another important activity of the travel agency. Some of the larger travel agents maintain sizable shipping an dforwarding departments, aimed at ssisting the traveler to transport personal effects and baggage to any part of the world with a minimum of inconvenience.

The multifarious activities mintione in the abpove paragraphs show that the travel agency range of services in modern times has expanded a great deal. The field of expertise is quite large and is constantly growing with the fast changing travel needs of the people. The job description of a modern travel agency can be summed up in the following words.

a. Preparations of individual pre-planned itineraries, personally escorted tours and group tours and sale of pre-paid package tours.
b. Making arrangements for hotels, motels, resort accommodation, meals car rentals, sightseeing, transfer of passengers and luggage between terminals and hotel and special features such as music festivals and theatre tickets.
c. Handling of and giving advise on the many details involved in modern day travel. E.g. travel and baggage insurance, language study material, travelers cheques, foreign currency exchange, documentary requirements (visas and passport) and health requiremtns ( immunization and inoculations)
d. Possession of professional knowledge and experience, as for instance, schedules of air and train connections, rates of hotels , their quality, whether rooms have baths, etc. all of this is information on which the traveler, but for the travel agent, will send days or weeks of endless phone calls, letters and personal visits.
e. Arrangements or reservations for special interest activities such as conventions, conferences and business meeting and sport events etc.

### 5.9 TRAVEL ORGANISATION

There are various activities which a travel agency has to perform in order that an intending traveler undertakes his proposed journey and enjoys a holiday of his choice. There are various steps involved from the time a traveler visits a travel agent to buy a ticket until he returns back home after visiting a place of his choice.

Organised travel by a travel agency can be of tow types, i.e. (i) Single client, and group client in order to effect the journey, the following main elements (in both types of travel) need to be considered.

a. study of the journey
b. Estimate of expenditure
c. Execution of the journey and carrying out
d. Presentation of accounts.

### INDIVIDUAL OR ORDINARY TRIPS

The following steps are involved in organizing individual or ordinary trips

i. The client turns to the travel agent to organize for him a particular journey (cultural, natural, business, religious, etc)
ii. The agency from this angle will examine as to what will be involved, e.g., scope of journey, when the journey is to take place, various services needed and the accessories required.
iii. Based on the abnove evaluation and other elements in his possession, the travel agent will suggest itinerary and will then communicate to the client the estimated maximum cost for the client's approval.
iv. The travel agent will then compile the definite estimates, a total off a series iof various costs added up, eg., transport, operatives costs such as (postage, telex, telefax, E-mail, telephones, etc)
v. The travel agent then will present a document of the amount of money to be paid in duplicate to the customer. The client rreturns one of the debniot copies signed on acceptance accompanies with a deposit (in anticipation). The deposit normally is about 25 percent of the total cost.
vi. Once the clients approval has been obtained, the travel agent operation department.
vii. Issues the vouchers.
viii. The travel agent prepares the tourist itinerary, which will accompany the client through the entire journey. It will indicate the tickets to be used; the hotel and other services booked and will include vouchers, etc. Normally the itinerary is made in triplicate one for the client, another for the agency and the third the hotelier or those who will provide the required services paid by means of vouchers.
ix. The last formality is the delivery to the client of the vouchers, confirmed tickets, and the technical itinerary.
x. When the group is particularly large, e.g., for sports etc., the travel agent needs to take an extra care by way of informing public authorities for purpose of security, etc.

Travel agents in a highly developed market cover all the above activities and range of services. The range of activities of a travel agent in any country depends upon the extent of the economic development of that country, the travel patterns of the population in advance countries and people with high incomes resulting in availability of disposable incomes for holidays, taking more holidays as compared to I developed countries. The services of travel agents are increasingly utilized in developed countries. In some of the advanced countries like the USA, Canada, Germany and Japan a very large percentage of tourists are utilizing the services of a travel agent.

## 5.10 HANDLING A CLIENT – WATA GUIDELINES

The agent's role in handling a client is very important. Once a client enters the agency it becomes necessary for an agent to properly anticipate his needs ad requirements. The client also has come with a pre-determined notion about a destination his visiting. WATA, the world association of Travel agencies, has prepared comprehensive guidelines for handling a client. These guidelines are based on the WATA master – key an annual publication of the world association of travel agencies. Updated and published yearly, the WATA master key is a selectively comprehensive source of travel information. Individual agency tariffs given in the publication represent the selling tool for members, incoming and outgoing services. Along with the tariffs the master key gives a country description in addition, the master key also gives detailed information bout some hotels located in important cities and tourist centers together with prevalent confidential tariffs and other relevant information for travel agencies.

The WATA Master key is valuable reference material for travel agents. Its presentation makes it easy for the users to extract the information they need. The guidelines as enumerated in the master key are as follows.

1. SALE OF A TOUR

It should first be determined whether the client who wants to book a tour prefers to:

Join and escorted tour, or

Choose a FIT, combining leisure and activity according to his individual tastes and interests.

2. FIT / YOUR RELATIONS WITH CLIENT

If your client wants a "tailor made" tour, let him make the suggestions, without imposing your own views, on the following points:

- Itinerary
- Determine the cities to be visited.
- Number of days (overnights) in each place.
- Mode of transportation between cities.
- Establish a rough time schedule, taking into consideration the time at his disposal

NOTE: For a leisure trip, it may be justified to convince your client to leave out some places which he can visit another time.

b. Transportation

1. Air transport should be used when time is limited and for long distances.
2. Surface transportation should be recommended for shorter distances.
3. For trains, determine whether advanced reservation is necessary. Indicate stations where trains are to be changed.
4. Bus should be recommended in some countries, as it usually allows additional sightseeing.
5. When arranging timetables, remember that your client is on vacation and therefore avoid early departures.

c. **HOTEL ACCOMMODATION**

1. Category of Hotels: Examine with your client category of hotel he wants to stay at Deluxe, first Class, Standard or Economy class. It is preferable that he is accommodated in a maximum rate room; however, if he must consider the cost, then rather suggest a lower grade hotel with best available room.
2. Type of rooms: Examine whether your client wishes a special room on a special floor, with or without bath / shower, sea view, outside or inside, etc. Draw his attention to the fact that in high season a room with a bath may be difficult to obtain in some places. In some cases a double room for single occupancy can be suggested a single room being often small or not well situated. If your client insists on havein a particular room, he may have to pay a supplement.

3. Meals: Ask your client whether he wants to have accommodation on bed and breakfast, dimension or full pension basis. If accommodation is on bed and breakfast basis, keep in mind that in certain resorts or hotels demi or full pension is compulsory.

4. Check – in time: Remind your client that chieck –0 in time at hotel is usually after 12 noon. Immediate occupancy on early morning arrivals can be only be secured if the room is reserved for the previous night. If your client leaves late in the evening you may propose to him to pay for a additional night..

5. During periods of festivals, fairs or congresses, hotel space may to be available, rendering it necessary for your client to change the dates in those places; cabled hotel confirmation should therefore be suggested.

6. During periods, such as important festival and clients a minimum stay of 5-7 days may be required. The same is applicable to some winter resorts, where a minimum stay of two weeks is required at Christmas and New Year.

### d. **Transfers**

- The need of transfers upon arrival or departure results from the fact it is often difficult to find one's way at airport, stations with which one is not familiar.
- Transfers by agencies include internal meeting and assistance, accompanying clients (unless otherwise specified), porterage and transportation of 2 pieces of hand luggage per person between airport, station, bus or terminal and hotels or versa, as tip to driver, but it does NOT include trip to hotel porter.
- Type of vehicle varies according to cities, generally by private car or taxi / cab.
- Airport transfers are naturally more extensive, but also the most convenient ones.
- When opting for transfer from city air terminal, your client must know that there will be no assistance at the airport, that he will have to tip for baggage at the airport and pay for bus between the airport and the city terminal.
- Bus arrivals: Certain bus companies stop at the major hotels to drop or collect clients, the disadvantage of this being the client's dependence of time schedule and waiting for his turn to be dropped off. In addition,

it will be necessary for the client to contact the local agency if other services are not to be provided in that city.

### e.  **Sightseeing / Excursions / Tours**

1.  The advantage of arranging sightseeing in advance is that your client does not have to waste his time, queing up in the local agency. Also a balance can be established in advance between leisure time and sightseeing, as well as for tours of the city and countryside.
2.  Motor coach tours: Apart from the economic viewpoint there is the advantage of meeting other travelers, but clients, as pick-up is very seldom done on motor coach tours.
3.  Private Car Tours: your client is packed up at the hotel, has the choice of time of department and can stop wherever he like but this is the most expensive solution. In some places there are regular private car tours, or else sightseeing can be done on a seal – car basis.
4.  Hire of Private Car with Chauffeur

    a.  City hire – must be recommended to deluxe clients, whose time is limited between trains, boats or planes or who already know the city and want to see only special places or go shopping. Since veryoften the chauffeur cannot act as guide, a private guide will be needed for sightseeing.

5.  Motor launch Tours / Boats Trips: The same applies have a motor coach tours. Deluxe clients will be picked up at the hotel by private car and driven to embarkation pier.
6.  Self – driven cars can also be provided when clients fill the necessary conditions and, if wanted, a local guide can be laced at their disposal.

**Music festival, Theatre and concert tickets:**
Clients must be told that advance reservation is necessary confirmation or requested tickets cannot be guaranteed and ticketsare no refundable unless they can be resold.

**QUOTATION**

·  Land arrangements

On the basis all details furnished by your clients it will enable you to make an estimate of land arrangements.

- Transatlantic / Pacific Transportation

To the land arrangements the cost of flight / boat tickets for transatlantic / pacific transportation has to be added.

- Cost price

Items a and b above you the cost price.

- Selling price

In order to obtain the selling price you should add your handling fees or make –up as well as a margin safeguarding any possible increase

**SUGGESTED ITINERARY**

a. A suggested itinerary should be drafted of what has been agreed with your client and submitted to him, together with the final price. The accompanying letter should clearly specify what is included in the price:

1. Price and type of land arrangements.
2. Price and class of air / sea / rail tickets, included, that they are subject to change without notice.
3. The agency's conditions regarding handling charge, cancellation fees, possible deposit request, etc.

- It should also point out what is NOT included, such as cost of passport, visa, gratuities, trips to hotel porters, beverages, laundry, taxes (government, landing, embarkation), etc.
- Acceptance of suggested itinerary should be requested to enable you to proceed with reservation, and a deposit should be asked.

*Market Research*

Market research is the systematic investigation of the facts relevant to various aspects of marketing. It helps in identifying the needs of the customers. It involves study of different markets and customers such as their tastes and preferences and what they are willing to buy and when they are likely to buy. It is a systematic collection of information relating to supply and demand for a product or a proposal. Identifying customer needs is very important especially in tourism business. Therefore, organisations involved in tourism business need to know who their potential tourists are, where they come from, their likes and dislikes, etc. so that a product can be designed according to their needs. This information will help an organisation to offer a product which can be effectively sold in the market.

## Product Planning and Development

Product planning and development is concerned with identifying customers' needs, developing new products and improving the existing products in order to meet the needs of customers. Tourism product is a composite product; it is the sum-total of a country's tourist attractions, its natural beauty, climate, history, culture, transport, accommodation and entertainment. Information collected through market research can help organisations to redesign existing products. For example a new tour package can be offered to a particular group of tourists.

Segmentation

Segmentation is a process of identifying groups of buyers of a total market with different buying needs or requirements. It identifies and analyses the socio- economic, life styles and motivational characteristics of potential buyers into useful categories and launches advertising and promotional campaigns for these selected groups. Segmentation helps tourist organisations to design and offer products to a particular segment as per the needs of that segment. For example, if a tourist organisation designs tour packages for religious tourists it means the organisation is providing a product for a particular segment.

Promotion

Promotion refers to a mechanism of communicating, to informing, persuading and influencing the customers to buy a product. The objective of promotion is

to make the customers aware of the product so as to create demand for the product. Promotion is the mix of various communication activities which tourist organisations carry out with a view to motivating or influencing the target customers. Various techniques that are used in promotion include advertising, publicity, personal selling, and sales promotion.

Selling

Selling is the process of helping customers to buy the products and services that an organisation offers at a price to earn profit for the business. The basic purpose of all marketing activities is to sell the goods and services. Selling helps the business to satisfy the needs of customers. A business can sell its products and services through the following selling methods.

Some common selling techniques are:

- Direct Selling - Salesperson sells directly to customers.
- Retail Selling - Products are offered through a shop that customers can visit.
- Agency Selling - An agent sells products and services on behalf of a supplier.
- Tele-sales - Products and services are sold directly on the telephone without face to face contact.
- Door to door selling - Salespeople visit potential customers at their homes and sell to them directly.
- Business to business selling - Businesses sell directly to other businesses.
- Mail order selling - Customers buy directly from a catalogue without seeing the product firsthand.
- Online Selling - Products and services are sold directly on the internet.

Marketing Mix

Once a firm has decided its overall competitive marketing strategy, it is ready to begin planning the details of the marketing mix. Marketing mix is defined as a set of controllable marketing tools that a firm blends to produce the response it wants in the target market. It consists of everything the firm can do to influence the demand for its product. It constitutes the core of the organisations marketing system which includes four basic decision areas known as the "four P's" of marketing .These are:

- Product,
- Price,
- Promotion, and

- Place (distribution)

These are four controls which have to be used very carefully by a marketing manager to achieve organisational goals. An organisation's success depends on good formulation of its marketing mix. Each of the four P's include many important sub-elements. **Product** is the heart of marketing mix and speaks about its unique features. It also includes pre-sale and post-sale services and the satisfaction it provides to the customer. **Price** signifies the value of a product. A desired quality with a reasonable price would attract the customers. **Place** refers to the place and time. It stands for activities undertaken by the firm to make the product accessible and available to target consumers. Finally **Promotion** speaks about how to improve sales with the help of various activities such as advertising, personal selling, sales promotion etc.

A best mix of above variables like right product at a right price, at a right place with a right promotional activity would yield the best results for a product. Since tourism and its related activities constitute service, the marketing mix for tourism, like any other service, would have three more elements in addition to these four P's; which create a new dimension in their marketing strategy. These include

- (1) People,
- (2) Physical Evidence and
- (3) Process.

People

As the people are involved in offering services to customers, their performance plays a vital role in tourism sector. The behaviour and attitude of the service personnel in a hotel, transport or a travel agency plays a key role while performing the services which are visible to the tourists. They play an important role in attaining customer satisfaction.

Physical Evidence

The common element in all services including tourism services is that they are tangible, physical, and controllable aspects of any service sector. Physical evidences can be used to build a strong association in the mind of tourists and also to differentiate the service from that of competitors. This element relates to the external and internal appearance of any tourism related organisation. For example, the customer in a restaurant would look for hygienic food in addition to the external and internal appearance of it.

Process

The tourist would look at the quality aspect in a service apart from the process time. A quick service with a quality is always preferred by a customer. If a tourism firm fails to satisfy this, a customer would switch over to the competitor who serves the tourist better. Thus, an efficient process, which would reduce the customer time without deteriorating the quality, should be adopted by a tourism organisation to retain the tourists.

## 5.10 DISTRIBUTION CHANNELS IN TOURISM INDUSTRY

A distribution channel is considered to be a vehicle that is utilised to make a product or service available to the consumer. The concept of distribution channels is not limited to the distribution of physical goods. Although the principles are the same, the channel distribution for tourism differs significantly from those used for manufactured goods. Tourism services require simultaneous production and consumption, meaning the product is not normally 'moved' to the consumer. A tourism distribution channel may be defined as a total system of linkages between actual and potential tourists and the suppliers. Distribution in tourism is transfer of tour and related facilities from supplier to tourists through a system. Distribution channel is used for indirect selling and it involves all those who are providing the product from the supplier to tourist. The following distribution channels are used in tourism.

Travel Agents

Travel agents are those who buy the product from wholesalers and sell the product to tourists for a commission. Travel agents act as intermediaries between the customer and the supplier and are known as retailers in tourism. Travel agents work in close contact with the tourists and build a personal rapport with the tourists. These agents act as a single local contact point and as such them need not contact many suppliers. Travel agents in some cases make all the arrangements at the destination and also simplify payment in case of international travel.

### National, State and Local Tourism Agencies

All travel agencies cannot provide all inclusive packages to their clients in all parts of the world. So these agencies promote tourism in certain geographic areas. They may be sponsored by the state or constitute business associations with the common goal of providing information and promoting tourism in certain regions. Tourist agencies advertise resources and tourist attractions, and help customers to plan their trips providing maps, guides, and bookings.

### Tour Operators and Wholesalers

Tour operators are wholesalers, also called consolidators, who buy in large volumes and have access to a surplus inventory on highly discounted rates. Tour operators prepare tour packages and give them to travel agents for selling. They design packages as per the requirements of the market. The wholesalers obtain rates and availability directly from the supplier and create packages with different accommodation and transportation options.

### Online Travel Companies

The use of Internet has given birth to new intermediaries also known as cybermediaries. These companies do not physically own the products, they buy from suppliers then display and offer products through internet. The examples of such companies are *m*akemytrip.com, yatra.com, cleartrip.com and ibibo.com.These companies sell tourism products like air tickets, railway tickets and hotel rooms etc.

### CRM and Tourism (Hospitality) Industry

Application of CRM in the tourism sector is in its early stage of development. Practical use of CRM can be seen in the case of hotels or hotel chains, which actively collect the available data about their guests. All available information about a guest is stored in a separate database and is properly analysed and a profile of each guest is created. Based on the created profile, it is possible to access each guest in a special and personalised way, because the hotel management and staff are familiar with the wishes and needs of guests. When the hotel has enough information about its guests, it can make classification and segmentation of individual guests or groups of guests, and can determine the product needs of each individual customer or group of guests.

# Reference

Reference and Source

https://nios.ac.in/media/documents/tourism_337_courseE/337

https://www.tutorialspoint.com/tourism_management/
tourism_management_tutorial.pdf

https://www.researchgate.net/publication/
302139257_Tourism_Management

https://www.nios.ac.in/media/documents/tourism_337_courseE/
337_Tourism_Eng/337

https://www.skylineuniversity.ac.ae/pdf/tourism/
Tourism%20Impacts.pdf

https://nibmehub.com/opac-service/pdf/read/Tourism

https://www.academia.edu/43451181/Tourism_Management

http://www.eiilmlibrary.com/library

https://hindustanuniv.ac.in/assets/pdf/ug/BBA_Travel_Tourism.pdf

https://backup.pondiuni.edu.in/sites/default/files/Tourism

https://hindustanuniv.ac.in/assets/pdf/ug/BBA_Travel_Tourism.pdf

Thank you Google.com